D0899009

THE DIAGNOSTIC PROCESS IN MEDICAL PRACTICE

THE DIAGNOSTIC PROCESS IN MEDICAL PRACTICE

MICHELE GROVES

Nova Biomedical Books
New York

Copyright © 2008 by Nova Science Publishers, Inc.

All rights reserved. No part of this book may be reproduced, stored in a retrieval system or transmitted in any form or by any means: electronic, electrostatic, magnetic, tape, mechanical photocopying, recording or otherwise without the written permission of the Publisher.

For permission to use material from this book please contact us:
Telephone 631-231-7269; Fax 631-231-8175
Web Site: http://www.novapublishers.com

NOTICE TO THE READER

The Publisher has taken reasonable care in the preparation of this book, but makes no expressed or implied warranty of any kind and assumes no responsibility for any errors or omissions. No liability is assumed for incidental or consequential damages in connection with or arising out of information contained in this book. The Publisher shall not be liable for any special, consequential, or exemplary damages resulting, in whole or in part, from the readers' use of, or reliance upon, this material.

Independent verification should be sought for any data, advice or recommendations contained in this book. In addition, no responsibility is assumed by the publisher for any injury and/or damage to persons or property arising from any methods, products, instructions, ideas or otherwise contained in this publication.

This publication is designed to provide accurate and authoritative information with regard to the subject matter covered herein. It is sold with the clear understanding that the Publisher is not engaged in rendering legal or any other professional services. If legal or any other expert assistance is required, the services of a competent person should be sought. FROM A DECLARATION OF PARTICIPANTS JOINTLY ADOPTED BY A COMMITTEE OF THE AMERICAN BAR ASSOCIATION AND A COMMITTEE OF PUBLISHERS.

Library of Congress Cataloging-in-Publication Data
Groves, Michele.
  The diagnostic process in medical practice / Michele Groves.
      p. ; cm.
  Includes bibliographical references and index.
  ISBN 978-1-60456-323-8 (hardcover : alk. paper)
  1. Diagnosis. 2. Medical logic. I. Title.
  [DNLM: 1. Diagnosis. 2. Logic. 3. Problem Solving. WB 141 G884d 2008]
  RC71.G852 2008
  616.07'5--dc22
                              2007049401

Published by Nova Science Publishers, Inc. ✤ *New York*

Contents

Preface

The selection of reliable and valid methods for evaluating clinical reasoning is a critical step in the delivery of the medical curriculum. This is especially so given the widespread introduction of integrated, problem-based learning (PBL) curricula in medical schools over the last two decades. In contrast to more traditional, discipline-based courses, in which acquisition of clinical reasoning expertise tended to be haphazard and heavily dependent on the nature and quality of the individual student's clinical experience and supervision, PBL places formal emphasis on the teaching and development of medical problem-solving skills. There is, therefore, both a need for these skills to be formally assessed and for the method of assessment to reflect the philosophy and method of tuition. The purpose of this book is to examine the nature of the clinical reasoning process, its development in relation to clinical expertise and the methods available for its assessment and evaluation.

Chapter 1

Introduction

In these days of increased consumer expectations and escalating healthcare costs, the ability of doctors to understand and diagnose patients' problems accurately and efficiently is more important than ever. This requirement is highlighted by the current focus on safety and quality and attempts by hospitals and health care providers throughout the world to reduce the high incidence of iatrogenic patient injuries. In the past, there has been a tendency to view these "adverse events" as a regrettable but largely unavoidable consequence of the uncertainty that surrounds medical practice. However, several recent studies have found that, not only do adverse events have a substantial impact on both patients and health care systems but many are highly preventable [1-4]. One large-scale Australian study found that 16.6% of hospital admissions are associated with adverse events leading to disability and/or increased hospital stays [4]. The great majority of these were judged to be the result of human error, with cognitive failure leading to missed or delayed diagnosis and treatment constituting the second largest cause of adverse events overall [5]. Furthermore, adverse events due to flawed diagnostic decision-making were more highly associated with preventability, permanent disability and death [4]. These findings emphasise the importance of the diagnostic process in the delivery of quality medical care.

In making a diagnosis, doctors are required to demonstrate both knowledge and reasoning skill. Clinical reasoning (or medical problem-solving) is a complex process that involves interaction between cognition, biomedical knowledge and clinical experience. In contrast to problems in non-medical domains, medical problems are often initially incomplete and poorly defined. They are also highly context-dependent. This implies not only that the solution (diagnosis and management) of a patient's problem may be difficult to achieve but also that the problem itself may be difficult to identify in the first place. Not surprisingly therefore, evidence suggests that the difference between strong and weak diagnosticians, lies in the level of their clinical reasoning skill as well as in the size, quality and accessibility of their knowledge base [6-8].

The development of clinical reasoning skill is an ongoing process whose foundations are laid during undergraduate medical education and which continues after graduation and throughout clinical practice. Consequently, it is imperative that undergraduate medical education places strong emphasis on both the teaching and assessment of clinical reasoning.

The selection of reliable and valid methods for evaluating clinical reasoning is therefore a critical step in the delivery of the medical curriculum. This is especially so given the widespread introduction of integrated, problem-based learning (PBL) curricula in medical schools over the last two decades. In contrast to more traditional, discipline-based courses, in which acquisition of clinical reasoning expertise tended to be haphazard and heavily dependent on the nature and quality of the individual student's clinical experience and supervision, PBL places formal emphasis on the teaching and development of medical problem-solving skills. There is, therefore, both a need for these skills to be formally assessed and for the method of assessment to reflect the philosophy and method of tuition.

The purpose of this book is to examine the nature of the clinical reasoning process, its development in relation to clinical expertise and the methods available for its assessment and evaluation.

Chapter 2

Reasoning and Medical Problem Solving

Early research into the nature of reasoning and problem solving viewed diagnosis as a categorisation task in which the patient's clinical features are grouped into an appropriate disease category. It assumed that problem solving skills were generic in nature and transferable between knowledge domains [9, 10]. This assumption underlay research in the fields of information processing, decision theory and categorisation which focussed on the fundamental elements of reasoning, such as the role of cognition and meta-cognition and the use of knowledge in searching for the understanding that enables decision making and intervention to occur [6, 11-13]. It was this work that established the importance of reasoning ability in problem solving and consequently, that skill in clinical reasoning is critical to the accurate diagnosis of medical problems.

However, in contrast to non-medical fields in which problems tend to be well-structured with all relevant information available from the outset (e.g. chess or physics), medical problems are frequently ill defined, with complex goals, and outcomes that may be ambiguous and difficult to predict. Cultural, domestic, work and socio-economic factors mean that information about a patient's problem may be fragmentary, inconsistent or inaccurate. Additionally, it is unusual for all the relevant information to be available on initial presentation [11]. Rather, it unfolds over time, which makes both formulation of the problem and its diagnosis and management complex and difficult [14]. This means that diagnosis is an inferential process in which the doctor must make a series of judgements about the patient's problem based on his/her presentation and clinical findings [15]. Furthermore, the complexity of the diagnostic task indicates that it is the effectiveness and efficiency of the clinician's clinical reasoning that determines how well medical knowledge is translated into patient care [16].

Sound clinical reasoning partly relies on the appropriate use of a range of generic problem solving strategies and types of reasoning. These allow the clinician to formulate the patient's problem in his mind and elicit, interpret and integrate clinical information as it becomes known. Three commonly used types of reasoning are probabilistic, deterministic and causal reasoning.

Probabilistic Reasoning

This type of reasoning is based on the statistical relationship between clinical variables and estimates the likelihood of a particular disease or disorder in a given patient [17, 18]. Probabilistic reasoning allows doctors to make diagnostic and management decisions independently of their pathophysiological knowledge. It is also useful in determining the likelihood that the benefits of treatment or further investigations outweigh potential risks. Implicit in the probabilistic approach is recognition of the need to restrict the degree of uncertainty to within acceptable limits [19, 20].

Accurate and acceptable probability estimates require a rigorous definition of disease and involve consideration of factors such as the prevalence of the disease in the patient population, the reliability of laboratory results and the sensitivity and specificity of the tests performed [21]. The probabilistic approach provides an explicit means of data interpretation, helps in the generation of diagnostic hypotheses by considering the relationship between a hypothesis and its prevalence, and emphasises principles of diagnostic testing. However, it has some significant shortcomings which limit its use in problem solving to a supplementary role. Firstly, it requires an exhaustive list of differential diagnoses. It assumes that each disease is mutually exclusive of all other diseases under consideration and that all clinical features are present throughout its course. Finally, it is unable to deal with the many test results which occupy the grey area between normal and abnormal [18].

Deterministic Reasoning

This uses predominantly compiled knowledge that has been formulated as unambiguous "production" rules. Production rules extend the definition of compiled knowledge to include basic units of cognition that specify both a condition that needs to be met and a consequence of satisfying the condition and thus, have an "if… then…" format [22]. They function as a framework for the development of mental models of disease, eliminating the need for a complex storage system of previously-experienced instances, the formulation of a therapeutic approach or appreciation of prognostic implications. Two common problem solving strategies based on applied deterministic reasoning are a) heuristics and b) algorithms, schema and flow charts:

a) *Heuristics* are mental short cuts or rules-of-thumb that reduce the number of questions that must be asked and the number of investigations to be performed, thereby making the whole task more manageable and efficient [23, 24]. The type of heuristic used depends on the level of expertise and the nature of the problem. Experts tend to use a strong diagnostic approach that enables them to conceptualise the problem, gather relevant data and apply a pre-compiled solution [25-27]. In contrast, novices and non-experts tend to use a non-selective search (direct questions about the problem) and scan (routine screening questions) approach, such as the systems review, which covers a broad spectrum of possibilities but which is less likely to produce high-quality hypotheses [25, 26, 28, 29].

b) *Algorithms, schema and flow charts* are employed to interpret single clinical findings. Providing they are accurate and the problem relatively simple, they ensure that the clinician covers all essential steps in the diagnostic process, and provide rapid and efficient solutions. However, there are considerable risks associated with their use:

- because of interaction between diseases, they are unsuitable for multiple pathologies or complex problems [18];
- they are unable to deal with uncertainty;
- they may be based on personal experience or opinion rather than experimental data or rigorous clinical observations and may thereby lead to invalid or defective solutions;

- they are context-dependent. That is, when applied to the same initial finding in a different context, they may produce two different, and not necessarily correct, solutions;
- their application or the result may be ambiguous.

Causal Reasoning

Causal reasoning is based on a cause-and-effect relationship between the disease and/or its clinical features and the underlying pathophysiology [15, 30]. This kind of reasoning enables a customised model to be created for each patient and can be applied at several stages in the diagnostic process – to formulate the problem, to explain unexpected findings, to eliminate competing hypotheses by assessing the strength of the links between cause and effect, to assess the coherence of the diagnosis once it has been made as well as the credibility of the entire chain of events leading to it [30]. In turn, the strength of the links is determined by factors such as the time period between stimulus and response. Causal reasoning is exclusively dependent on biomedical knowledge and takes no account, either by definition or in reality, of epidemiological factors, such as the incidence or prevalence of the disease, or the particular context of the patient's problem.

Causal reasoning is a powerful tool for many reasons. By relying on basic science principles, it is able to explain variability in findings, to explain findings which cannot be understood by probability estimates or comparison with a known pattern, and to unite the various clinical features into a common framework. It is also able to confirm the validity of probability estimates (e.g. two features may be equally likely to be present in a disease, but only one of them may have a causal link) and provide a pathophysiological basis for treatment.

Consequently, probabilistic, deterministic and causal reasoning can be seen as complementary to each other with all having a role to play in diagnosis, depending on the nature and complexity of the problem. Although causal reasoning is exclusively dependent on biomedical knowledge of structure and function and independent of the patient population, it is the most powerful since it provides an explanatory model founded on the use of basic science principles. Nevertheless, deterministic reasoning, although less dependent on detailed biomedical knowledge, is an efficient means of solving routine, straightforward clinical problems as also is probabilistic reasoning with its focus on population and disease demographics. Additionally, both probabilistic and deterministic reasoning provide the context within which causal models operate [18].

All of these types of reasoning are elaborated in the clinical reasoning process used by doctors to diagnose patients' problems. However, a sound reasoning process is necessary but is not sufficient of itself for expertise. Diagnostic expertise is also heavily knowledge-dependent. How knowledge is organised in memory, and how it is integrated with the reasoning process determines the level to which clinical expertise develops. In the next section, the clinical reasoning process will be discussed in relation to the nature and development of expertise.

Chapter 3

The Nature and Process of Clinical Reasoning

Historically, diagnostic reasoning has been considered an art, an intuitive ability that cannot be taught but which emerges only after considerable clinical experience. It has been observed that such expert reasoning is rapid and almost unconscious; it involves switching between search and scan strategies with no noticeable change in behaviour on the part of the doctor [31]. Furthermore, it is seen only in real-life settings where the exigencies of practice frequently mean that responsibility for the patient's future well-being rests solely with a clinician operating in an environment where there is insufficient time for full and leisurely consultation [32].

Reasoning Strategies

In order to understand and solve a diagnostic problem, it is necessary first, to recognise that a malfunction or abnormality is present in the patient, and second, to identify its cause. The diagnosis therefore, can be considered as an explanation (often causal) of the disordered function achieved through the exercise of knowledge, reasoning and judgement. Often, additional information is required so that inferences may be drawn about the underlying pathophysiology [33]. Observations about the cognitive phenomena associated with the diagnostic process have resulted in the formulation of two widely recognised strategies of clinical reasoning, both of which use the same hypothesis-driven approach but which differ in the type of knowledge that is used. The two strategies are hypothetico-deductive reasoning (HDR), predominantly used by non-experts; and pattern recognition, used by experienced (expert) clinicians.

Hypothetico-Deductive Reasoning

HDR exemplifies a generic approach to problem solving which originated in medical research [11, 12, 27]. It is based on the generation of multiple hypotheses early in the patient encounter. Such hypotheses are triggered by the identification of cues or key features in the patient's initial presentation [12] prior to the collection of any additional data. Hypothetico-deductive reasoning, in the form of problem-based learning (PBL) which mirrors and elaborates on the diagnostic process, has been widely adopted as the most useful approach to teach diagnostic skills to medical students in the early years of their undergraduate training.

At the beginning of a consultation, the patient presents the clinician with various verbal and non-verbal cues such as his appearance, dress, age, manner, the nature of his symptoms and possibly, prior knowledge about his personal circumstances. The cues that the clinician selects as important enable him to form an initial concept (or mental representation) of the patient's problem. Almost simultaneously, several hypotheses are generated to explain this concept. Hypotheses are not necessarily diagnostic entities in themselves but may represent anatomical, physiological, pathophysiological or aetiological explanations of the problem. As such, they can range from the extremely non-specific ("a heart problem") to the highly specific ("left ventricular failure") [16]. They can also describe the problem in different ways eg. as an infection, a clinical disorder or syndrome or as a specific disease [12, 15, 27].

The early generation of hypotheses serves four functions:

- it begins the process of imposing structure on the problem where none previously existed;
- it increases the efficiency of the diagnostic process by proposing a small number of possible solutions, thus limiting the breadth and scope of the problem (the "problem space");
- it allows the selective acquisition of further data through history-taking, physical examination, laboratory and other investigations; and
- it provides a model against which a patient's findings can be assessed [14].

Each hypothesis can be used to predict the additional signs and symptoms that should be present if the hypothesis is true, meaning that the second stage of the diagnostic process is a guided search for specific additional data. Interpretation of the additional data allows existing hypotheses to be prioritised and refined or eliminated, and new hypotheses to be generated if necessary. Thus, a continuing process of hypothesis generation, testing and refinement is established which leads to eventual diagnosis [34].

Hypotheses are refined in parallel with each other rather than sequentially – an approach that increases efficiency and makes both premature elimination of a particular hypothesis and bias towards a "favourite" hypothesis less likely. Refinement proceeds via a search and scan technique. Searching comprises deliberate questions or tests, the results of which allow the clinician to deduce which hypotheses are most likely. Scanning questions are used if he/she reaches an impasse in the search and are designed to identify new cues or data, enabling further hypotheses to be generated and/or existing ones to be re-prioritised. Scan questions are usually functional enquiries about organ systems (the "systems review"), the patient's background or medical history [34].

As information about the problem accumulates, its significance is assessed in relation to the generated hypotheses and added to the initial problem concept or representation. This allows the clinician to form a clear picture of the *status quo* at various stages of the consultation, to use it to assess the coherence and adequacy of each hypothesis with respect to the patient [27] and to eliminate competing hypotheses [26]. The final stage is closure, the decision-making component of the clinical reasoning process, which occurs whenever the clinician feels he has adequately understood and evaluated the patient's problem and is ready to commit to a treatment and management plan [32].

Hypothetico-deductive reasoning has been criticised on the grounds that it is really only applicable to problems with a single pathology in which all the clinical features can be explained by one diagnosis [35]. Its critics argue that a more methodical approach, as exemplified by Clinical Problem Analysis (CPA) [35] and the University of Calgary's scheme-based clinical presentations [36], may be more effective in providing novices and students with early problem-solving skill. Both these approaches are modifications of hypothetico-deductive reasoning and remain firmly hypothesis-driven. CPA operates after the identification of relevant features and initial hypothesis generation and focuses on refining each hypothesis by thorough analysis of each relevant feature. While this process encourages the use of basic science knowledge and provides a systematic, if rather ponderous, method of reaching a working diagnosis, there is a risk of so fragmenting the problem that the ability to integrate all its elements into a coherent solution may be lost (i.e. "missing the wood for the trees"). Scheme-based clinical presentations also provide a more structured approach and emphasise the technical aspects of clinical problem solving rather than providing a conceptual basis on which the clinical reasoning process can be developed. Both represent a retreat from the less didactic and more student-centred approach considered to be one of the more desirable and effective aspects of hypothetico-deductive reasoning and PBL.

Nevertheless, in the health professions, hypothetico-deductive reasoning is considered the dominant model used, to varying degrees, by novice and expert practitioners alike [14, 37]. It involves both inductive reasoning (to generate hypotheses) and deductive reasoning (to test and refine them). Understanding of the problem occurs as a result of ongoing interpretation of data in the light of the clinician's existing knowledge.

Pattern Recognition

Pattern recognition is a reasoning strategy which allows rapid, efficient and accurate diagnosis. It is characterised by direct automatic retrieval of stored knowledge [38, 39] and is triggered by identification of key features within the case [17]. Because it is predominantly used by experienced physicians working on routine or familiar cases [13], pattern recognition has been proposed as a model of the cognitive processes of experts. The characteristics of pattern recognition suggest that there is a strong association between expert reasoning and knowledge, not only with regard to the size of the knowledge base, but also to its organisation and accessibility. In other words, with experience, the reasoning process becomes automatic, implying that expertise in clinical reasoning develops in line with the evolution of the clinician's knowledge base from one which is highly conceptual to one in which this knowledge is integrated with experiential knowledge. This process entails continuous knowledge re-structuring and re-organisation and culminates in a knowledge base that includes stores of previously encountered instances and exemplars (or prototypes) and the clinical patterns that the clinician has derived from them [10]. The outcome is a clinical reasoning process characterised by a non-analytic and almost unconscious ability to recognise and manage familiar situations. As a form of expert reasoning, pattern recognition is also heavily context-dependent and qualitatively different from the clinical reasoning of novices [40].

Pattern recognition occurs in two forms – instance-based categorisation and prototypes. Because both are frequently discussed in terms of how knowledge is structured in memory, they are described briefly here prior to a more detailed examination in the discussion of models of knowledge organisation.

- *Instance-based Categorisation:* each new case is classified according to its resemblance to previously experienced cases or clinical patterns by recognising similarities between them and the clinical features of the new case [8, 41]. Consequently, it is also referred to as instance-based recognition [8]. Instance-based categorisation is strongly influenced by context - the non-medical aspects of a case which include social, cultural and personal factors. This suggests that correlation is with specific previous cases, rather than with an abstraction of several cases; and that there is an associative link between the context in which a disease occurs and the events or circumstances surrounding previously experienced cases in that disease category.
- *Prototypes* are based on the concept that knowledge of a disease category is naturally structured around clear examples, or prototypes, which capture its essential meaning and contain its most commonly occurring features. On each occasion that the disease is encountered, the clinician abstracts its central concepts and uses these abstractions to develop a prototype of that disease category. Thus, the content and structure of prototypes is a function of clinical expertise [6, 39]. Recognition of subsequent instances of the disease is matched against the learned abstractions, rather than specific instances (as in the categorisation model) and results in an increased ability to interpret clinical data [42].

It has been generally accepted [8, 39, 43, 44] that these two cognitive strategies, pattern recognition and hypothetico-deductive reasoning, provide substantial evidence that the thought processes of novices and experts are intrinsically different. However, Barrows and Feltovich (1987) have argued that, regardless of the level of clinical expertise, some form of hypothesis-driven reasoning is involved in every case because pattern recognition can only operate *after* the clinician has identified and accumulated at least some, if not all, relevant data. They further contend that pattern recognition ignores the complex mental processes which occur while the case is unfolding, and is only applicable to particular specialties where temporal unfolding of data is not an issue, such as dermatology and radiology, where all (relevant and irrelevant) information is present from the outset. Acceptance of this proposition means that the process of pattern recognition should be regarded as a highly evolved form of reasoning that has been honed and made efficient through practice and experience, thereby allowing unconscious, automatic associations between hypotheses and the investigative strategy needed for diagnosis [45]. Further support for such a view is provided by the observation that experts generate competitive and highly relevant working hypotheses, which are then refined by focussed, "high yield" inquiries [46]. This feature is lacking in novices because of their relative lack of clinical experience [16].

Process-Content Integration

Consistent with research findings in non-medical fields [47], studies in medical problem-solving have shown that clinical reasoning is not a separate capability which can be learnt independently of relevant knowledge and professional skills [8]. The importance of an organized, discipline-specific knowledge base in clinical reasoning is now well-recognised [6, 13, 48-51]. Consequently, it seems likely that the most realistic representation of how doctors think during the diagnostic process is a hybrid of both hypothetico-deductive reasoning and pattern recognition [39, 52]. This conclusion suggests that hypothesis-testing with its associated deductive reasoning, is explicitly used not only by non-experts but also by experts when dealing with unfamiliar cases, while prototypes and inductive reasoning are used to generate hypotheses and/or diagnoses. Rapid problem classification, a characteristic of experts, consists of a mixture of pattern recognition, hypothesis testing and intuition [53] (where intuition includes the ability to identify abnormal presentations of familiar diseases as well as the key features critical to accurate diagnosis [54]). An important implication of this proposition is that clinical reasoning depends on the doctor's perception of the problem's characteristics and complexity which in turn, depends at least partly, on the knowledge and experience of the doctor him/herself [55].

However, recognition that diagnostic skill is dependent on both sound reasoning and knowledge is comparatively recent. Initial research into clinical reasoning was predicated on the assumption that medical problems were relatively homogeneous with respect to the skills required to solve them. Therefore, there should exist a generic problem solving process that could be universally applied. The suggestion was that not only could doctors solve problems across all knowledge domains, once they had mastered this process, but that any deficit in the knowledge required to solve the problem would be acquired during the learning and practice of the process itself.

While the hypothesis-driven process that underlies all forms of clinical reasoning does provide some evidence for the existence of such a generic approach, further research found that its effectiveness was not related either to the clinical skill or the experience of the practitioner. That is, it was unable to explain differences between strong and weak diagnosticians [12, 42, 56, 57]. In fact, the strongest predictor of accurate diagnosis was shown to be choosing the correct hypothesis in the first place [57]. Other process variables, such as the quality of the hypotheses generated, the type and quantity of data gathered, and the accuracy of the diagnoses made, were unrelated to level of clinical problem solving skill, as measured by techniques including simulated patients [58], patient management problems [59] and computer simulations [60]) and to vary depending on the nature of the clinical case [12, 58, 59]. In other words, expertise is content-specific [12, 61] and dependent on the knowledge base [62, 63], and experts are only experts within their own domains of specialisation. Furthermore, it was found that the development of clinical reasoning is not a linear progression, but is characterised by a "dip" in diagnostic performance at the intermediate level of expertise [64-66]. These findings forced researchers to consider the possibility that the differences between expert and novice diagnosticians owed more to knowledge and its organisation in memory than to the application of generic problem solving strategies, as had been previously assumed [12].

This realisation resulted in a seismic shift in research into the diagnostic process away from the process-oriented approach and towards a content- or knowledge-oriented approach. This change of focus resulted in the emergence of a content-oriented perspective which contends that reasoning and knowledge are interdependent and that therefore, effective problem solving also requires an appropriate store of relevant knowledge [67-69]. Researchers in this area argue that, because problems in the human sciences (such as medicine) are not discrete and their solutions not necessarily definite or even clearly defined, practitioners operate in a world of uncertainty which requires a concept of knowledge that incorporates interpretive ability and the exercise of professional judgement [69]. This concept of knowledge is founded on three principles [70]:

- knowledge is a human construct that seeks to make sense of the world in which an individual finds himself (also known as constructivism);

- much of the knowledge required for effective health-care is dynamic, imprecise and context-dependent;
- modern professionals need personal knowledge or wisdom in addition to practical knowledge.

These principles inform current understanding of how knowledge is structured in long-term memory, and accessed during the diagnostic process. Attempts to explain how knowledge is used in the clinical reasoning process have lead to the formulation of a number of models which focus on the organisation, storage and retrieval of knowledge from memory.

Knowledge Organisation

Cognitive psychology views diagnosis as a categorisation task in which the patient's clinical findings are fitted into a disease category [71, 72] with each category containing individually necessary and jointly sufficient, critical features that define the disease. However, this approach does not allow for the inherent variability of disease presentation, which means that frequently, one or more of the so-called critical features may be absent without affecting the validity of the diagnosis. This, combined with the realisation that reasoning alone was unable to discriminate between strong and weak diagnosticians [12], challenged the view that diagnostic expertise only required mastery of the reasoning process and an adequate knowledge base [16, 42, 73] and suggested that clinicians' knowledge must be organised in a way that enables them to maintain the identities of diseases as individual concepts despite the potential variability of clinical findings.

How knowledge is organised in memory influences clinical reasoning in at least four ways:

- it allows clinical findings to be formulated into a semantic construct [6];
- it identifies and establishes connections (including causal links) between sets of findings and enables the development of abstract concepts [74];
- it accommodates newly acquired knowledge, thereby elaborating existing constructs and deepening understanding [8];
- it superimposes clinical patterns derived from experience and embeds them as integrated entities into memory [17].

As a result, three representational models of knowledge organisation incorporating these influences were developed that are specifically applicable to medical diagnosis - prototypes [6], instance-based models, and semantic networks, schema and scripts [7, 75]. Each model is discussed below.

Prototypes

The classical view of organisation of knowledge is that it is criterion-based, i.e., the criteria for a disease category, such as anaemia, are identified and assembled into a list of disease sub-types. This approach implies that all diseases in a category share some common features, are equally good representatives of the category and that inter-category boundaries are clear and distinct [6]. However, there is evidence that knowledge of a disease category is naturally structured around clear examples or prototypes, which contain the most commonly occurring features of the disease, and that not all features are necessarily present in all examples of the category [76].

Prototypes are developed using an abstraction process to construct common memory traces of two or more patients with the same disease [77]. They can be considered either as a set of weighted features [76] or as the definitive example of the disease or patient [78]. Variants of the prototype model include Bayesian models which focus on probabilistic relationships between clinical features and disease category [79]. Prototypes have an intuitive appeal because they enable patients and diseases to be defined in terms of the typicality or otherwise of their clinical features, rather than whether or not the features are definitive. That is, they are flexible and realistic. They are also able to explain why clinicians prioritise features on the basis of their typicality and frequency of occurrence [6]; and why typical patients are diagnosed quickly, accurately and confidently [80].

The prototype model assumes that each feature of a disease contributes separately and independently to its prototype. This is not necessarily true since features may be co-dependent. As a result, the impact of two or more features together may be more or less than the sum of their individual contributions, thereby altering the power of the prototype to produce an accurate diagnosis. As well, the complexity of many medical cases questions the actual notion of features. Clinical findings, such as "moderately depressed" or "poor nutritional condition", require experienced medical judgement and are significantly more context-dependent than factual features, such as temperature, blood pressure or pulse rate [81]. In other words, in addition to proficiency in abstraction, personal attributes such as judgement and experience, are necessary to learn a category. Finally, the prototype model does not explain why it is possible to predict the consequences of a condition (such as an untreated infection) which is more likely to be based on theoretical knowledge than abstraction of prior experiences.

Instance-Based Models

These models view disease knowledge as collections of individual examples in which the integrity of each is preserved rather than its individual features being abstracted and assembled into one idealised example, as occurs with prototypes [71, 81]. Thus, learning simply involves the addition of successive instances to the knowledge base, and means that the independent nature of the features is preserved and the context of a case is integral to each instance [75]. It also allows for the continual re-interpretation of previous instances in the light of later experiences.

Instance-based models are able to explain three phenomena of the diagnostic process which are not accounted for by prototypes:

1. The reliance of many clinicians on previous instances even when other modes of categorisation (such as rules) are available and there may be only one previously experienced instance to guide categorisation [82, 83].
2. The influence of context in predisposing clinicians to form different concepts of the same disease, thereby leading to possible errors in diagnosis [84]. That is, an "atypical" context may lead to mis-categorisation and a wrong diagnosis even if the case is highly typical with regard to its clinical features.
3. The preservation of each example or instance in its entirety explains why several complex features are able to be processed as a single integrated entity [78] and why previously encountered, although atypical, stimuli are sometimes processed faster than new prototypical stimuli [85].

Both instance-based models and prototypes function well as mechanisms of pattern recognition. However, as models of knowledge organisation, they lack discriminatory power since neither explains the basis for a feature's inclusion or exclusion in a disease category. For example, a clinician may see 10 cases of stroke, all of which involve a 45 year old male with black hair driving a red sports car. The prototype model stipulates that irrelevant features (black hair and red sports cars) be included in the disease category of stroke as well as relevant features (age and gender). In contrast, application of the instance-based model significantly increases the probability estimate that a 45 year old male with black hair and a red sports car has suffered a stroke, even if the clinical findings point overwhelmingly to an alternative diagnosis [75].

Semantic Networks, Schema and Scripts

These use the connection between structure and function to explain how knowledge is used to reach a solution. Knowledge is seen as a network of single concepts or nodes connected by a variety of links, which may be causal, temporal, contextual or associative in nature. Initial activation of one or more nodes occurs in response to an external stimulus with further activation of the network spreading selectively via the links.

According to this model, diagnosis can be considered as the process of finding a path through a network of medical knowledge to the node which represents the disease category, using a case's clinical features as a guide. The most important attribute of the semantic network model is that it is able to accommodate the process of clinical reasoning rather than just a yes/no recognition of prototypes or instances. Often, semantic networks are seen as applying to biomedical knowledge while schemas and scripts are seen as representations of clinical knowledge [8, 66] which have been developed through the repeated application of clinical experience [86], even though the connection between the two may be sub-conscious and unrecognised.

Schema are defined as knowledge structures whose purpose is the efficient achievement of an objective. Scripts are more developed forms of schema which allow for the timing and location of particular events [7]. A disease script consists of a set of clinical features (attributes) each having a default value which qualifies the attribute. For example, a script for acute appendicitis may contain attributes and default values such as acute onset, severe lower abdominal pain and low grade fever. It is important to note that it is the relationship between the features rather than the features themselves that are exclusive to the script. That is, abdominal pain can also be an attribute of a script for bowel obstruction, but it will not have the same relationship to temperature and onset that it does in acute appendicitis nor will its default value be necessarily the same [87].

This model of knowledge organisation supports the hypothetico-deductive approach to clinical reasoning. The first step in the clinical reasoning process, identification of relevant cues in the patient's presentation, triggers the activation of multiple scripts. That is, an activated script is equivalent to a hypothesis [50] and provides one of several possible interpretations of the case. Script processing involves the clinician actively searching for the patient's values for each attribute in the script and equates to hypothesis-testing. The correct script (or diagnosis) is the one which best accommodates the patient's clinical features, i.e. has the least difference between its attributes and values and those of the patient [87].

Both schema and scripts develop either as a direct consequence of the spread of activation or through the imposition of additional structure (via new knowledge) on an elementary nodes-and-links network [66, 86]. For example, the repeated simultaneous activation of two or more linked nodes leads to the development of new more complex nodes as knowledge is elaborated, and to the formation of sets of nodes clustered around a specific domain or topic. These are sometimes referred to as "chunks". A chunk is defined as "a meaningful pattern of information encoded in memory" [88]. Chunking allows information to be processed more rapidly and in larger steps [89]. Large scale chunking results in the development of schema or scripts as sub-sections within the network [90] and also, almost inevitably, the uneven development of the network. (This may go some way towards explaining case specificity – a feature of expertise that will be discussed in the following section.) Hence, schema and scripts can be viewed as generic constructs that are able to represent an instance of any illness [87].

The principal shortcoming of the semantic network model lies in its inability to explain why individual knowledge structures (including scripts in particular) show little overlap or consistency with each other [91]. That is, it does not explain the idiosyncratic nature of knowledge representation. Nevertheless, semantic networks are more widely applicable than the prototype and instance-based models because they are able to link medical knowledge to clinical reasoning at different levels of expertise. This model also explains why clinicians do not necessarily misdiagnose the first case of a disease category they encounter [92], as would follow under both the prototype and instance-based models. Specifically, semantic networks allow for a return to basic principles and concepts in the reasoning process, even if such a process is neither the preferred option nor the most reliable means of diagnosis.

In conclusion, it seems likely that clinicians have all three models available to them and coordinate their use, either in combination or singly, depending on the nature of the case and the level of clinical expertise. For example, semantic networks may be more appropriate in cases which emphasise specialised knowledge, such as endocrinology where causal relationships are essential to understanding and diagnosis [93]; instances may be more applicable to cases where the patient's background or context are important; and prototypes may be more useful in the diagnosis of low variance, high frequency diseases [41]. Similarly, instances and prototypes may be more consistent with the expert's use of pattern recognition while semantic networks are in greater accord with the non-expert's reasoning through a case via elaboration and consolidation of their knowledge.

In order to fully understand the role played by these models in clinical reasoning and the diagnostic process, a large body of research has emerged which focusses on the characteristics which differentiate novice from expert behaviour. The following section examines what it means to be an expert and the cognitive changes which occur during the development of expertise.

Chapter 4

Clinical Expertise

The Nature of Expertise

The *Oxford English Dictionary* (OED) defines an expert as one who has been "trained by experience or practice, (is) skilled, skilful" and "whose special knowledge or skill causes him to be regarded as an authority; a specialist". So the first thing that can be said about experts and expertise is that theoretical knowledge alone is insufficient, that expertise requires both experience and skill. But is practice, skill and theoretical knowledge all that is required? What is the difference between expertise and competence? Referring to the OED once more, "competent" is defined as "suitable, adequate, or sufficient, in amount or extent", "sufficient but not going beyond this" and "possessing the requisite qualifications". That is, competence also requires skill, practice and knowledge but there is a sense that the competent person is somehow less than an expert. So, the question becomes one about the true nature of expertise. What are the attributes of an expert that differentiate him from the merely competent? Guest et al suggest that not only the amount but the quality of time spent in practising a skill is one distinguishing factor [94]. To attain and maintain the highest possible standard of performance, deliberate practise is needed - both to improve the requisite skills and to allow different approaches to be explored. Implicit in this approach is that deliberate practice also requires that the practitioner's level of theoretical knowledge be maintained and constantly updated.

A second distinguishing factor derives from the nature of the task to be performed. Deliberate practice may be sufficient for static tasks which involve mastery of technical skills, such as playing the piano or measuring blood pressure, but not for dynamic tasks. Dynamic tasks have an inherent fluidity which requires flexibility and adaptability on the part of the practitioner. An obvious example in medicine is the task of diagnosis because some or all of its components (patient, context, clinical features) and even the task itself, vary on each diagnostic occasion. The clinician must be able to think and act "on the hoof" by devising strategies appropriate to the particular situation and adapting them as the demands of that situation change. That is, the dynamic expert must have problem-solving skill in addition to technical skill. As mentioned above, technical skill can be achieved through deliberate practice but deliberate practice in problem-solving, especially in fields such as medicine, is more difficult to acquire. This is due not only to the dynamic nature of the task, but also to ethical considerations which require clinicians to deliver the best possible performance at all times, and which largely prohibit them from exploring alternative approaches to treatment and management. One way to overcome these limitations is to constantly monitor and reflect on one's performance. This meta-cognitive ability is the third, and possibly most vital, factor that distinguishes the expert from the competent practitioner. Moreover, the ability to revisit previous experiences and reflect on the associated thought processes and activities (that is, to make the most of an experience) requires both motivation and personal insight [95].

In conclusion then, it can be said that there are four criteria for the achievement of expertise: maintenance of an up-to-date knowledge base, deliberate practice, adaptability and meta-cognition. As well, these criteria require motivation on the part of the practitioner to accept and overcome the challenges of their particular area of specialty rather than to limit the scope of their practice to their existing abilities [94]. However, having established the pre-requisites for expertise, the next question is to ask in what ways expert performance differs from that of novices. In other words, what are the characteristics which distinguish the expert from the novice?

Expert Characteristics

Experts in any field have certain characteristics in common [96] which, when applied to specific disciplines, are qualified by factors unique to that discipline. This is particularly true of medicine where it has been demonstrated that clinical expertise is associated with the following characteristics.

Expertise is Case Specific

Evidence suggests that the difference in the problem-solving process of experts and novices lies, not in the nature of the process itself, but in the quality of its application [12, 56, 57, 97]. That is, experts "do it better" in that they are more likely to identify relevant information, generate more accurate and specific hypotheses, use more focussed questions to refine them and to provide a more coherent explanation of the case. However, regardless of the level of problem-solving ability, and although it has been shown experts and novices also differ in the breadth and integration of their knowledge content, correlation across problems is low at all levels of expertise. This suggests that clinical reasoning is "content specific" [12]. That is, the solution of a clinical problem requires knowledge specific to the problem, and this knowledge is sufficiently variable to inhibit consistency of performance across problems [58]. This finding accords with general studies on knowledge transfer that show that there is a limited relationship between cognitive ability and generalizability of problem solving skill [47].

While relatively little research has been done on the nature of content specificity, there is intuitive appeal in the notion that an expert is so simply because he knows more about a specific area of knowledge than does the non-expert. Consequently, it has been assumed that the lack of generalizability of research findings on problem-solving ability reflects differences in knowledge content. However, if lack of generalizability was solely due to this, it would be expected that:

i)   tests of content knowledge would show low correlation across specialties or knowledge domains but this is not so [98].

ii)   there would be greater correlation within domains or specialties than between them since there is more overlap of the specific knowledge required to solve related problems than there is for the solution of problems in different specialties. However, a number of studies have failed to show an association between knowledge and overall problem solving performance regardless of the method of knowledge assessment used [12, 58, 59, 61, 99-101].

One possible explanation for these findings is that problem solving performance depends on the reasoning strategy used by the clinician. But what factors determine the choice of strategy? Research in cognitive psychology [98] has shown that the transfer and application of knowledge acquired in one context, to the solution of problems in other contexts, occurs through a process known as *analogous transfer*. Analogous transfer involves the recognition that specific acquired knowledge is both suitable and useful in solving conceptually similar problems. The process involves representing the (new) problem in a way that facilitates selective retrieval of a previously encoded analogue (or instance) and adapts the solution procedure from that analogue to the needs of the problem [102]. It is based on the notion that all problems have a hierarchical content organisation, ranging from its concrete details to the abstract description of its solution [103], and three dimensions:

1. context, which includes both the physical setting and the implied goals;
2. content, including a semantic domain (eg, pathophysiology of the cardiovascular system) and surface elements (eg, the presenting features);
3. deep structure or schema, which signify the underlying concept (eg, ischaemia).

While there may be similarities at the levels of content and context, true analogies occur at the deep structure level [104]. Because novices lack the discipline-specific knowledge to discriminate between critical and non-critical findings, they tend to identify similarities in surface features only. Hence, any change in these from one problem to the next impedes transfer [105]. In contrast, experts are able to identify common relationships between problems that enable them to develop schema based on generalisations of basic concepts, thereby allowing more accurate assessment of the nature of the problem.

Schema can be developed either by *abstract induction* in which principles and concepts are induced by abstracting a general (and therefore context-independent) rule [106] or by *conservative induction* in which the developed rule is context-dependent, and experts have the same rule available in several different contexts [107]. Abstract induction is a similar process to that employed in the development of prototypes and is a common feature of traditional medical curricula whereas conservative induction is one of the principles of PBL curricula – that concepts induced and learned in one context can be de-contextualised and applied to other problem settings. The ability to transfer concepts across contexts results in the development of internal schema individually adapted for every problem encountered and is an expert characteristic [98]. In this sense, schema can be compared to the production of instance scripts, in which a patient's clinical features replace the default settings of the more generic illness scripts.

In summary, case specificity may be explained by both the amount and quality of knowledge, and the extent of analogous transfer from the knowledge base to the problem. Although the extent of transfer is highly dependent on both the knowledge domain and the context of the problem, selection of the solution strategy is determined by the degree of similarity of the underlying concepts [108, 109].

Experts' Problem Representations Are More Meaningful and Conceptualised than Non-Expert

When a clinician first begins to gather information about a patient's case, he forms a mental representation of it that contains a perception of the elements of the patient's problem, the relationship between them, and a clear idea of the desired outcome of the problem solving process [7, 110]. Mental representations facilitate both understanding and access and retrieval of relevant knowledge. Their creation entails transforming the patient's signs and symptoms from the raw form in which they are first presented into abstract clinical terms known as semantic qualifiers [111]. Semantic qualifiers are categorisations of information into opposite ends of a continuum that describe clinical findings from a number of different perspectives, such as time course (gradual-sudden), location (peripheral – central) or quality (dull-sharp). Their development is a consequence of both organisation of knowledge and depth of understanding gained from personal experience [86]. Semantic qualifiers act as keywords in the search for appropriate prototypes or illness scripts stored in the clinician's knowledge base. As well, by representing a problem in this way (that is, as a set of clinical findings held together by semantic associations), the deep meaning of individual signs or symptoms can be fully understood and used to generate and test appropriate hypotheses [112]. However, while there is evidence that more weight is given to clinical features expressed as semantic qualifiers and other forms of "medicalese" (e.g. expressing "shortness of breath" as "dyspnoea") and that this is related to diagnostic accuracy, it is not known whether this is partly due to the use of medical terminology or whether it is simply that strong diagnosticians tend to represent cases in this way [113].

When dealing with a patient's case, a clinician's knowledge base operates at three levels: the patient's signs and symptoms, his own repertoire of potential diagnoses, and his mental representation of the clinical findings expressed as semantic qualifiers [111]. Bordage and his colleagues have used semantic analysis to clarify the way clinicians represent problems during the clinical reasoning process [74, 111, 114]. They have identified four semantic classes of knowledge organisation which correlate with level of expertise [112]:

i) *reduced:* clinical reasoning shows no connection between the problem and the knowledge base. This may be due either to poor organisation of knowledge or to an actual lack of knowledge [112]. Few or no semantic qualifiers are expressed [114].

ii) *dispersed:* although individual signs and symptoms generate multiple hypotheses, these are not tested by reference to the findings or in the context of the overall clinical picture, and new findings trigger new hypotheses rather than refine or eliminate existing ones [115] This suggests that, whereas the quantity of knowledge may be more than adequate to the task, it is poorly organised and results in a trial-and-error search for the correct diagnosis. Few or no semantic qualifiers are expressed [114]. Dispersed knowledge tends to feature collections of facts, lists, etc. that have been acquired through rote learning.

iii) *elaborated:* the patient's signs and symptoms are predominantly expressed in abstract terms as sets of opposing semantic qualifiers that directly link the characteristics of the problem (mode of onset, severity, location, context, disease category, pathophysiology, etc.) to the clinical findings via semantic networks, resulting in an elaborated problem representation. As a consequence, clinical reasoning is focussed, pertinent and clear, and the comparing and contrasting of competing hypotheses is facilitated.

iv) *compiled:* there is a more concise and coherent expression of large numbers of semantic qualifiers than at the elaborated level. The overall pattern of clinical findings is recognised [16] and associated with a complex, compiled semantic term [112] which expresses an encapsulated concept (e.g. sub-lesional symptomatology) [8, 86]. The process is rapid and dynamic, and entails checking the findings against those expected from the pattern [115] and noting and evaluating any discrepancies [112]. As expertise develops, the use of such encapsulations become more prominent [116]; knowledge becomes structured around prototypes and pattern recognition is the dominant form of clinical reasoning

Semantic analysis has indicated that one of the components of the difference between weak and strong diagnosticians lies not only in the use of semantic qualifiers to organise the way they think and represent cases, but also in the quality of the semantic qualifiers themselves [117]. The strongest diagnosticians are able to organise signs and symptoms into a more diversified and coherent system of related abstract qualities, thereby acquiring a broad and deep understanding of the problem. In contrast, weak diagnosticians are unable to recognise the semantic qualities of the presentation. This is reflected by measures of diagnostic accuracy which show that 75-80% of elaborated or compiled problem representations result in the correct diagnosis compared with nearly zero for reduced or dispersed representations [112].

There are three other areas where expert problem representations differ from those of non-experts. Firstly, the representations of weak diagnosticians are characterised by associative and conditional relations [115] based on deterministic or probabilistic reasoning. These relations imply that a particular finding is the result of the presence of some other finding (and therefore resemble the "if... then..." rules referred to earlier) but give no causal explanation and thus operate at a more superficial level of understanding. In contrast, expert problem representations are coherent with causal links between findings and diagnoses. Secondly, the expert's problem space is more evenly dispersed so that there is minimum overlap both between and within categories of disease, allowing more accurate differentiation between them [117]. Thirdly, because the expert's semantic relations are more diverse and abstract, his associated prototypes are more content-rich and complex [114] [74]. Therefore, he is more able to identify the interrelationships between findings and potential diagnoses, as well as any additional information required [118].

Experts Have Superior Recall of Diagnostically Relevant Information

When interpreting clinical information, both novices and experts identify personally important features in the case. These "forceful" or "key" features activate specific knowledge structures that promote the understanding and interpretation of clinical findings [119]. The number of key features identified by novices and experts is usually not significantly different. However, those identified by experts are qualitatively different and highly diagnostic compared to those identified by novices [27, 32]. These differences are directly related to diagnostic accuracy [48] and level of expertise. They are also inversely related to case difficulty. This was first demonstrated by Grant and Marsden when they presented 75 subjects whose level of expertise ranged from first-year medical students through to consultants, with four paper-based cases, two of which were straightforward and therefore classified as easy and two of which were more complicated and difficult. Each case was written to contain 10 items of clinical information (or clinical features). Subjects were asked to give a maximum of five possible diagnoses and to identify the items that lead them to each diagnosis. Results showed that, regardless of the level of expertise, fewer features were identified and fewer diagnoses proposed in the difficult cases compared to the easier ones [50]. Furthermore, the quality of the hypotheses that are generatedalso diminishes in inverse proportion to the degree of difficulty of the problem [49].

These findings suggest that the differences in the clinical reasoning process of experts and novices are due to modifications in the relevant knowledge structures that occur as a result of repeated activation. The extent and nature of the modifications depend in turn, on the amount and quality of clinical experience. Thus, these changes are unique to the individual. As knowledge structures become more and more individualised [50], an increasingly idiosyncratic clinical reasoning process develops which is based on personal relevance and utility [120]. Although this implies that there may be multiple paths to a problem's solution, the very concept of expertise argues against the notion that these paths are equally efficient or even correct. However, it does suggest that there are strong links between key features and disease groups in the expert clinician's memory that permit the rapid retrieval of knowledge. Rapid knowledge retrieval explains another feature of clinical expertise – the generation of hypotheses early in the patient consultation [27, 32] and indicates that accurate diagnosis requires recognition of the sets of attributes or key features that characterise a disease category, and the deduction of appropriate inferences from them [48]. In this sense, key features may be considered as components of prototypes and scripts.

The Development of Clinical Expertise Is Not Linear but Is Characterised by a "Dip" in Diagnostic Performance at the Intermediate Level

The relationship between expertise and clinical reasoning adopts an inverted U-shape on some criteria for expertise (e.g., recall of case detail and identification of relevant data) but not on others, such as diagnostic accuracy [64-66]. This *"intermediate effect"* contradicts studies in non-medical disciplines [121, 122], which show that the more expert a person is, the more knowledge he has about a subject, and the more detail he will recall when given new information about it. In one of the first investigations into the origin of the intermediate effect, Schmidt showed that, while diagnostic accuracy was consistent with the subjects' level of expertise, both the amount of detail recalled and the pathophysiological explanations of subjects at intermediate levels of expertise (advanced medical students or junior doctors) were consistently more elaborate and extensive (but less selective) than those of either novices or experts [65]. These findings are supported by other similar studies [123-126]. In practical terms, this means that junior doctors develop more extensive differential diagnoses [127, 128] and tend to order many more investigations [129]. Although they eventually reach the correct diagnosis, it is a relatively inefficient process because they have yet to develop the ability to discriminate between relevant and irrelevant data. This dip in performance also occurs whenever new knowledge is being acquired, especially if this involves the superseding of existing knowledge [130].

The intermediate effect can be considered as specifically related to the development of dynamic expertise. As stated earlier, expertise involves both mastery of static skills and the development of an adaptive ability to deal with the complexity of dynamic tasks. Patel [131] suggests that medical expertise follows a pattern of more-or-less continuous learning of higher order knowledge interspersed by periods of "processing" in which the newly acquired knowledge is organised and integrated into the existing knowledge base. It is during this updating, restructuring and enrichment of the semantic network that the intermediate effect occurs. This implies that maintenance of expertise itself is a dynamic task, regardless of the nature of the specialist domain or task (static or dynamic).

The Expert's Knowledge Base is Characterised by the Dynamic Integration of Biomedical and Clinical Knowledge

Cognitive theory states that problem solving requires integration of knowledge across disciplines and that this occurs as the result of the construction of links between them [13]. These links are created at three levels and reflect depth of understanding:

- at the surface structural level, through identification of similarities between domains;

- at the intra-domain level, through recognition of analogies in conceptual causal relations;
- at the inter-domain level, through association of abstract concepts and relations in one domain to more concrete concepts and relations in another.

In medicine, biomedical knowledge is applied differentially depending on the level of expertise [127]. Novices focus on the surface similarities between domains, indicating superficial learning. Intermediates, who have minimal experience but abundant theoretical knowledge, focus on analogies. Although analogies are based on higher level relations, intermediates commonly misapply the causal links, resulting in wrong or inconsistent inferences. Experts, on the other hand, are able to identify abstract concepts and relations across domains which allow them to generalise [132].

There has been considerable debate and confusion about the role of biomedical knowledge in clinical reasoning which is only now being resolved. It is clear that increasing expertise is strongly associated with the level of development of knowledge organisation [133] and increasing diagnostic accuracy [127, 134, 135]. However, evidence suggests that experts, when presented with a clinical case, predominantly use clinical knowledge to represent and diagnose the problem; and that it is novices and intermediates who actively apply biomedical knowledge to its solution [44, 136]; [86, 114]. This implies that the use of basic science principles is a characteristic of non-expert reasoning [65, 136]. Paradoxically, there is also support for the traditional belief that biomedical knowledge provides the basis for understanding a patient's problem and that expertise is associated with flexible and more appropriate use of biomedical science [7, 137-139]. This implies the existence of a deeper understanding and explains the diagnostic accuracy which is one of the hallmarks of clinical expertise. More recent research, based on case representation methodology, has shown that, in the absence of time constraints, experts are in fact, able to explain clinical cases in basic science terms [140]. Other studies have confirmed that experts have well-developed biomedical knowledge that is accessible at all times but that it is only activated if needed to diagnose a difficult or atypical case or if time is unconstrained [48, 93]. In routine circumstances or when time is limited, experts provide (elaborated) summaries of the case which bypass biomedical concepts and directly link its signs and symptoms to high level clinical concepts (e.g. ischaemia or inflammation) [140].

Additionally, experts' explanations of the pathophysiology underlying a problem are more coherent, precise and detailed than those of non-experts [13, 134] and correspond more directly to the problem [86, 137, 138]. These findings extend to experts' problem representations which are more coherent and contain fewer biomedical concepts and more clinical knowledge than those of non-experts [115]. This inverted-U shaped relationship between the amount of biomedical knowledge applied to a problem's solution and level of expertise represents another aspect of the intermediate effect. Students at the intermediate level of expertise have a relative absence of clinical experience and predominantly use biomedical knowledge to find the diagnosis [65, 141, 142]. The associated lack of coherence in their explanations reflects the lack of an adequate clinical science "scaffold" from which to hang their biomedical knowledge [143]. Finally, the clinical reasoning of novices, whose basic science knowledge is incomplete and clinical knowledge almost non-existent, is characterised by widespread errors and inconsistencies [135, 141, 143].

The ambiguity of these results suggests that the relationship between applied knowledge and diagnosis is more complex than previously imagined and that it is modified as a result of clinical experience. Indeed, as expertise increases, the structure and function of both biomedical and clinical knowledge changes, leading to a decrease in the *overt* use of biomedical knowledge and an increase in the application of clinical knowledge [86]. These changes are a consequence of two factors that suggest that the role of biomedical knowledge in the diagnostic process is implicit rather than overt and explicit. These factors are the accumulation of experiential knowledge which directly links a patient's signs and symptoms to his diagnosis; and the repeated application of biomedical science in the early stages of clinical experience which causes its encapsulation and integration as coherent units into clinical disease knowledge [13, 144].

Thus, integration consists of three dynamic processes: the application of biomedical knowledge to the construction of a global framework; reflection on the relationship between clinical experience and the framework; and development of connections between them [145]. This explains how it is that experts' encapsulated biomedical knowledge remains viable and accessible for use in complex cases or when an explanation of the underlying pathophysiology is required [86, 142]. It also suggests that the primary function of biomedical knowledge is to structure seemingly unrelated phenomena into coherent, well-organised information [146] which is easily recalled and explained – an essential feature of clinical expertise.

Experts Make Better Use of Context

Biomedical knowledge is just one component of a clinician's disease knowledge. Another is the contextual features of a case that give it uniqueness. Contextual features primarily describe the patient's medical, social and work-related environment and include any risk factors for disease, such as age, race, gender or weight, to which he may be susceptible, thereby influencing the probability of a particular diagnosis [8, 147, 148]. In this sense, the term "integration" also refers to the clinician's ability to integrate all aspects of a problem into his diagnostic reasoning, whether they are contextual, pathophysiological or clinical.

Apart from a patient's presenting complaint, very little explicit information is available in the initial stages of a consultation. Yet, it is well established that experts generate diagnostic hypotheses very early in the consultation (frequently before history-taking is begun) and that the quality and accuracy of these first hypotheses largely determine the accuracy of the final diagnosis [11, 56, 57]. Evidence indicates that experts take more account of implicit information (such as the patient's physical appearance and demeanour) than novices, even if this information is not overtly related to the presenting complaint [148]. Furthermore, recognising the significance of the contextual features of a case enables them to activate more appropriate clinical disease scripts [147-149]. This, at least partially, contributes to experts' greater diagnostic accuracy but also to the relative speed of their diagnoses [125].

These conclusions are further supported by research into the relation of visual cues to diagnostic accuracy [150-152] and into the relation between contextual features, speed of hypothesis generation and quality of hypotheses [153]. In both cases, it was found that experts are more sensitive to contextual features than novices, and this sensitivity increases the speed with which they are able to reach a diagnosis. Additionally, although hypothesis generation about the pathology underlying a patient's signs and symptoms occurs at all levels of expertise, experts also relate pathology to the problem's context [144] as well as to the presenting signs and symptoms. For example, severe abdominal pain in a child who has been winded in a rugby tackle suggests a different pathology from that occurring in a middle-aged female with a history of heavy periods. This strongly suggests differential development of components of clinical disease scripts which is not dependent on amount of knowledge about contextual features in general, but rather on the ability to apply this knowledge to a specific case [55, 154].

The central role of knowledge organisation in clinical expertise determines another performance-related feature of experts - the ability to solve problems quickly and correctly. In addition to a readily accessible knowledge base which allows a disciplined, logical problem-oriented search strategy, experts use heuristics to increase efficiency. These include the use of "high yield" questions that confirm or eliminate more than one hypothesis at a time. That is, experts get the right answer faster because they are able to limit the problem space by using inquiry strategies which yield the maximum amount of discriminatory data [32] and enable them to consider and evaluate several hypotheses simultaneously [32, 153].

Over and above these knowledge-related characteristics, experts have a well-developed meta-cognitive ability which gives them a self-awareness and insight into their own performance which allows them to monitor when and why they make errors, lack understanding or need to review diagnoses [96]. In addition, meta-cognitive knowledge enables the clinician to evaluate the diagnostic demands inherent in a clinical case and to devise strategies for diagnosis and management [155]. Thus, meta-cognition acts as an interface between general problem solving ability and discipline-specific knowledge [156], and provides a strategy for dealing with the variability, uncertainty and cognitive limitations inherent in clinical decision-making [52]. It also allows the clinician to plan, control and evaluate the knowledge and strategies used in clinical reasoning [51].

In conclusion, clinical expertise can be considered a consequence of the interaction between meta-cognitive ability, reasoning (as demonstrated by mastery of such problem solving strategies as hypothetico-deductive reasoning and pattern recognition) and a well-organised, discipline-specific knowledge base [37]. As a result of the relationship between knowledge organisation and expert characteristics, [8] proposed a theory on the development of expertise which is primarily based on the concept of the ongoing re-structuring of the knowledge base. This theory and some alternative approaches are discussed in the following section.

How Clinical Expertise Develops

In addition to experience and knowledge, effective doctors also require skill in diagnosis, communication and interpersonal skills, intuition, judgement, and personal qualities such as empathy and compassion. It has been argued that the most important of these factors in the delivery of quality care and management of patients is diagnostic strength which in turn, is based on sound clinical reasoning [34]. Clinical reasoning develops from the interaction of clinical experience and knowledge, and it is this interaction which at least partly differentiates between strong and weak diagnosticians. Furthermore, it is not simply the quantity of knowledge *per se* but also, and especially, its level of organisation in long-term memory that is the vital component in the interaction [6, 13, 48, 114, 157]. This finding, that level of expertise corresponds with the organisation and structure of knowledge, is acknowledged as a major factor in the performance differences between novices, intermediates and experts.

- In order to explain the different performance characteristics of novices, intermediates and experts, a single theoretical framework, the Stage Theory of Clinical Reasoning Expertise [8, 86], has been formulated. Stage theory emphasises the parallel development of clinical reasoning expertise with knowledge acquisition, and assumes that:
- the development of expertise is a continuum involving progression through several stages, each characterised by different knowledge structures/representations;
- these structures accumulate, remaining viable and available for future activation;
- experts routinely use knowledge structures (commonly referred to as illness scripts or patterns) derived from extensive and continued practice. Illness scripts contain little pathophysiological knowledge but a large amount of relevant information on disease, its context and consequences, and cover a broad spectrum from general disease categories to individual patient problems [158].

Stage theory identifies and describes four stages in the development of clinical expertise that are the result of progressive changes in knowledge structure: the elaboration of causal networks, encapsulation of knowledge, the emergence of illness scripts and finally, instance scripts.

The Development of Elaborated Causal Networks

When medical students first begin to learn biomedical information, they organise it into a structural network which consists of nodes (discrete concepts or units of knowledge) related to each other by causal links. In this way, the causes and consequences of disease are explained in terms of the underlying pathophysiological processes. This leads to the establishment of lines of reasoning which are able to relate diverse clinical findings, and which facilitate the generation of multiple hypotheses covering several organs or systems [159] that explain individual clinical features although there is little or no ability to integrate them in the initial representation of the problem [115]. However, as more knowledge is acquired, the network becomes larger with new nodes being added, existing ones refined, all connected by more and stronger links. That is, knowledge becomes elaborated [160].

Encapsulation of Knowledge

Once a student begins to apply his knowledge to clinical problems and to develop clinical knowledge, the links between relevant concepts in the causal network are activated. Frequent activation of the same links leads to "clustering" of concepts. Clustering promotes the formation of direct linkages between the first and last concepts in a line of reasoning and circumvention of the intermediate nodes. Knowledge clusters can be considered as encapsulating diagnostically relevant concepts that explain signs and symptoms. Such encapsulations function as mental short-cuts and can summarise entire pathophysiological processes. For example, the encapsulated concept "urine retention" can be used to explain several of a patient's symptoms and contains within it the associated mechanism:

Enlarged prostate → decreased urethral flow → increased bladder volume → bladder distension → symptoms including difficulty with micturition, discomfort and frequency [159].

There are two implications of this encapsulation process. First, encapsulations develop as a result of the student learning to discriminate between knowledge which is relevant to the case and that which is not. Consequently, they consist only of that knowledge which is used all the time, and this enables a solution to the problem to be more rapidly found [8]. Second, because it entails integration of biomedical and clinical knowledge, clinical reasoning at this point uses almost no basic science concepts. Instead, students are able to make direct links between clinical features and concepts (hypotheses or diagnoses), but maintain the capacity to "unencapsulate" when confronted with difficult or atypical cases [160].

The Emergence of Illness Scripts

Simultaneously with encapsulation, there is a change in the knowledge structure from a causal network to a list-like, associative network. This is a result of the gradual transformation of encapsulated knowledge into diagnostic labels or abstracted mental models that are able to explain clinical findings sufficiently to allow decisions to be made about diagnosis and treatment [8]. These models, termed "illness scripts", have three components whose interrelationship emphasises the importance of integration in the development of expertise:

i)   enabling conditions - the contextual features of a case. Enabling conditions are important determinants of the probability of a particular diagnosis [153];

ii)   faults – the underlying pathophysiology which links the enabling conditions to the patient's signs and symptoms; and

iii) consequences – the clinical features of the case.

Because illness scripts are abstract in nature, they can be compared to the prototype model of knowledge organisation. However, they have one important advantage – the presence of enabling conditions in their construction means that, in addition to causal links, contextual and temporal links are included within them [7]. Other noteworthy features of illness scripts are:

- a relative absence of pathophysiology except as a simple explanatory model, e.g. tissue invasion;
- a serial structure: components in the script occur in story form rather than in chronological order because the clinician tends to re-order the clinical data of a case to match the activated illness script [38, 71, 125];
- development entails the overlaying of formal conceptual knowledge of disease features with informally acquired perceptual knowledge, which consists principally of enabling conditions and the variability of features [159]. Thus, the composition and quality of illness scripts are absolutely dependent on both quality and quantity of clinical experience as well as the personal experiences of the physician [8];

- they are part of a larger conceptual structure and are linked to each other through common elements. The links are dynamic and can be changed and updated as a consequence of ongoing experience [161];
- they exist at all levels of generality from representations of general disease categories to specific diseases to individual patients [8].

The development of illness scripts differentiates expert clinical reasoning from that of novices and intermediates. Illness scripts function as integrated entities with all elements within them being simultaneously and automatically activated. In addition, script activation generates an expectation of the other clinical features a patient might have. This means that, when dealing with a patient's problem, the expert's clinical reasoning is a process of script search, selection and verification [8].

Instance Scripts

Instance scripts are a consequence of the verification process in which the patient's actual values or findings are slotted into the "default settings" contained in the activated illness scripts. Scripts which are unable to accommodate the patient's findings within certain limits, are de-activated and the corresponding hypotheses discarded. In this way, instance scripts act as supplements to illness scripts and are stored in long-term memory where they remain available for future reference as exemplars [6]. Therefore, the greater the clinical experience, the greater the number of instance scripts available for activation, the greater are the chances of a "perfect match" between a patient's case and a stored instance script, and hence, the greater the degree of clinical reasoning expertise. That is, there is a synergistic effect between the clinician's illness scripts and his set of instance scripts [8]. Instance scripts also allow for the inherent variability of clinical findings – each script "setting" is able to accommodate a defined range of values and the presence or absence of non-critical features [147]. In experts, these ranges are more refined and accurate than novices.

The degree of "fit" also influences the speed of diagnosis. Typical or routine cases in which the patient exhibits nearly all of the expected clinical findings, are diagnosed much faster than atypical cases which may not have a matching instance script available [162]. A corollary of this is that the more atypical a case, the greater is the likelihood that the wrong illness script was activated initially.

That is, the typicality or otherwise of a patient's signs and symptoms influences the probability estimate that he has a particular disease [153].

Stage theory assumes that all medical knowledge is organised as one vast network of encapsulations in which biomedical concepts and their causal links are subsumed under larger clinical propositions which are connected to each other by associative mechanisms [8]. That is, the network consists of many, not necessarily equally developed, sub-networks of clinical propositions, such as anaemia, each of which contains both clinical features and the underlying pathophysiology, all related by the appropriate causal or associative (deterministic or probabilistic) links.

However, Patel and Kaufman [163] argue that knowledge encapsulation is not a feasible model for three reasons. Firstly, physicians' explanations of a clinical case become increasingly abstract and contain fewer biomedical concepts as their level of expertise increases [136]. Secondly, although PBL integrates basic science mechanisms into a clinical context, students have great difficulty transferring and applying basic science concepts from one context to another [164] which suggests that biomedical and clinical knowledge are not integrated in long-term memory. Thirdly, biomedical knowledge is qualitatively different from clinical knowledge because it includes causal mechanisms and therefore requires a multi-levelled hierarchical structure rather than a network. Instead, they propose a "two-world" model [146, 163] in which they argue that this knowledge exists as two completely distinct networks – one composed of biomedical knowledge in which pathophysiological concepts (nodes) are connected by causal links and a second consisting of clinical knowledge in which concepts of disease are connected to signs and symptoms via associative links. That is, biomedical networks rely on causal reasoning and clinical networks on deterministic and/or probabilistic reasoning. They conclude that the role of basic science is to facilitate the coherent explanation of clinical features into a diagnostic finding, but that the biomedical knowledge network is only activated when the associative links of the clinical knowledge network are inadequate for diagnosis. That is, biomedical knowledge is invoked to "reason through" a clinical problem from basic science principles when the faster and less labour-intensive process of associative reasoning is unable to meet the demands of the task.

Both of these models are based on the belief that biomedical knowledge is only activated for atypical or rare cases. Yet, it has recently been shown that, in the absence of time constraints, experts are in fact, able to explain clinical cases in basic science terms [140]. This suggests that the structure of expert medical knowledge contains elements of both models and is organised as one network of interrelated biomedical and clinical concepts. Over time, the associative links between signs and symptoms, causes of disease and high level clinical concepts become much stronger than the causal links between clinical concepts and pathophysiological mechanisms, but there is no encapsulation, as such. It is argued that instead, the mechanism for this process involves the activation of all links related to the disease but that causal links between biomedical concepts and the consequences of disease require more time to be activated to the same degree as associative links [140]. Thus, if processing time is limited, only associative links between clinical findings, causes of disease and clinical concepts will be activated strongly enough to figure in the clinician's representation of the case [165, 166].

Extrapolating this view to script formation involves the concept of "chunking". A chunk can be considered to result from the development of strong associative links in the knowledge network. The concept of chunking overcomes the problem of unfolding encapsulated biomedical knowledge but still allows the type of rapid, automatic and non-analytical pattern recognition that is characteristic of expert clinical reasoning [58, 163]. In fact, Norman [167] defines expertise as "the ability to mobilise rapidly, a vast and inter-connected body of knowledge to solve a particular problem".

Regardless of the precise details as to how expert knowledge is structured, the most important implication of the stage theory, that expert clinical reasoning differs from that of novices because of fundamental differences in the way knowledge is organised in memory, holds true. Considering the development of expertise as a journey characterised by specific, uniformly experienced milestones linked by some form of transition mechanism explains many aspects of expert clinical reasoning not explained by the conventional approach to diagnosis as a purely problem solving exercise [8]. These aspects include:

Content specificity: Because a clinician's knowledge network is absolutely dependent on the type and frequency of clinical experience, its development is likely to be uneven. Frequently activated knowledge clusters will be transformed into illness scripts, while rarely activated segments of the network (such as biomedical concepts) will remain relatively under-developed. In other words, if experts depend largely on script-based knowledge which is idiosyncratic and experiential rather than pathophysiological in nature, diagnosis is likely to be based on the similarity between the contextual features of the case and previously encountered instances rather than biomedical knowledge [71].

Identification of critical data: Expert clinical reasoning is much more discriminating than novices in that experts identify significantly fewer clinical features as critical or essential data [57]. Illness scripts allow rapid and easy recognition of a problem based on its similarity to previous cases as well as predicting additional findings for confirmation. In contrast, non-experts need to use pathophysiological networks, activated by a relatively greater number of the patient's signs and symptoms, to confirm each aspect of the case.

Problem representation: As a result of the qualitative shift and increase in knowledge consequent on clinical experience, experts form a global representation of a patient's signs and symptoms as a whole, rather than as individual features. For example, novices and intermediates tend to explain symptoms such as fever, chills, sweating, prostration, shortness of breath, tachycardia, etc. individually whereas experts subsume these individual concepts into a single, higher level, clinical concept inferred from the case and recall these features as "a septic condition". Thus, stage theory explains why the recall protocols of experts are both sparser and more comprehensive than non-experts, why experts produce more inferences on recall despite their overall recall being less detailed [168] and why they explain cases largely in terms of clinical knowledge [143, 169].

The intermediate effect: Intermediate level subjects have a large active store of elaborated but relatively unstructured theoretical knowledge which lacks the experiential component required for script development [65]. Therefore, while they are able to explain the clinical features of a disease mechanistically, their reasoning is based on the conscious activation of less tightly organised, causal pathophysiological networks – a more time-consuming process than the expert's automatic activation of entire illness scripts. Patel and Groen [43] suggest that intermediates are unable to make a selective judgement about the relevance of patient findings and therefore access their knowledge indiscriminately, attempting to process all received information, whereas experts use scripts to filter out irrelevant data. They conclude that, rather than reflecting intrinsic differences in the nature of their mental processes or knowledge structure, the intermediate effect may simply be a strategy to cope with the demands of newly acquired knowledge that has yet to be processed, i.e. structured in memory.

Summary: Where Are We Now?

Clinical reasoning involves solving medical problems in order to make decisions about a patient's diagnosis and management. To do this, clinicians have available two well-recognised clinical reasoning strategies, namely hypothetico-deductive reasoning and pattern recognition. The choice of strategy depends on the nature of the problem and the clinician's level of expertise. In turn, expertise in clinical reasoning is largely a consequence of level of knowledge organisation.

An important consequence of this research, especially the discovery that hypothetico-deductive reasoning is unable to distinguish between strong and weak diagnosticians, was the invalidation of the traditional view that clinical reasoning was process-, rather than content-dependent. This finding not only helped to direct research towards the role of knowledge in diagnosis, it also prompted a re-evaluation of many of the techniques used to assess clinical reasoning and diagnostic competence.

The clinical reasoning process can be summarised as consisting of the generation of hypotheses (equivalent to the differential diagnosis) about a patient's problem which begins early and continues throughout the consultation. These hypotheses are developed from the identification and interpretation of certain key features in the presentation, history, physical examination and clinical investigations. As such, these hypotheses constitute a shifting population that is continually refined by the addition of new hypotheses or the elimination of invalid ones, until a working diagnosis is reached. In experts, extensive clinical experience results in this process becoming more sophisticated. Clinical reasoning is rapid, efficient and accurate and characterised by the automatic retrieval of stored knowledge in the form of scripts in response to particular clinical features.

In the remainder of this chapter, techniques that have been used to assess clinical reasoning and/or evaluate the clinical reasoning process are reviewed in relation to this concept of the reasoning process. Its implications for medical education curricula are examined and suggestions made about possible methods for accurately assessing the development of clinical reasoning during medical training.

Chapter 5

Measuring Clinical Reasoning

The notion of clinical competence incorporates three major components: clinical skills, which include the technical aspects of the patient consultation (communication, history-taking, physical examination), knowledge and diagnostic ability. A pre-requisite of diagnostic ability is proficiency in clinical reasoning. Nowhere is the difference between the process of clinical reasoning and the skill of diagnosis more apparent and more significant than in their assessment and evaluation.

General Considerations

There are several issues to be considered when deciding on a method of assessment, including reliability, validity, practicality, efficiency and cost. The most important of these are validity and reliability. That is, does the method measure what it is intended to measure and does it do it accurately and consistently? A method may be reliable without being valid, but it cannot be valid unless it is reliable [170].

Validity

Validity can be subdivided into several types, of which face, content, criterion-related and construct validity are the most important. With the exception of face validity, all give information about aspects of the method being used.

(i) *Face validity* indicates whether the method is seen by students and examiners as measuring the content to be assessed. It is not strictly necessary for a method to have face validity since it does not directly contribute to the effectiveness of the method in measuring a particular paradigm.

(ii) *Content validity* indicates the degree to which a method tests a representative sample of the examinable material or content. A test has content validity if it reflects both the content and the objectives of the material being assessed.

(iii) Criterion-related validity indicates the degree to which performance measured by one method is related to another measure of performance or criterion. There are two types: predictive and concurrent validity.

- *Predictive validity* indicates the ability of the test to predict future performance of some trait. For example, a method for testing clinical skill should be able to predict which students will subsequently become competent diagnosticians
- *Concurrent validity* indicates the extent to which a method produces the same results as those obtained using another established method (frequently referred to as a "gold standard") or criterion.

(iv) *Construct validity* indicates the extent to which a method measures a psychological trait or construct. Examples of such constructs are intelligence, critical thinking and motivation [170]. Assessing construct validity requires confirmation, not only of the constructs that a test measures, but also of those it does not measure. That is, construct validation is subject to multiple criteria amongst which are included all other types of validity since these also provide information which helps to establish exactly what a test or method measures

Reliability

Reliability is a measure of the reproducibility of a measurement and depends on several factors, including consistency in marking, format and length of testing, test content and quality of the method used [171]. As with validity, reliability can be classified into subtypes, namely test-retest (or external consistency), internal consistency, inter-rater reliability and inter-case reliability.

i)   *Test-retest reliability* indicates whether a test will give the same result if the test is applied in the same circumstances on two separate occasions. This is the most common measure of reliability in scientific research. However, this measure of reliability is not suitable for research in the social sciences for two reasons. Firstly, there may be a learning effect from the first time a test is taken, especially if the second test is taken shortly afterwards. Alternatively, if there is a significant period between assessments, there is the possibility of effects from intervening events, such as lectures and practical sessions.

ii)   *Internal consistency* is more commonly used in educational research. Internal consistency is a measure of reliability based on establishing whether each item in a test is measuring the same underlying construct, i.e. whether the items are consistent with each other. One parameter is Cronbach's coefficient alpha which is based on the concept of split-half reliability in which the items in a test are divided into two equal groups and the relationship between respondents' scores for the two halves calculated. Also known as the alpha coefficient, it is the average of reliability coefficients for all possible split-half combinations.[170].

iii)   *Inter-case reliability* measures consistency of performance across all items in the test. To ensure inter-case reliability, it is necessary that a test contains a broad sample of subject matter.

iv)   *Inter-rater reliability* measures the degree to which different examiners agree about test performance. Adequate briefing of examiners is needed to ensure acceptable inter-rater reliability.

In medicine, particularly in the assessment of clinical skills such as clinical reasoning and communication, the major issues of concern are construct validity, internal consistency and inter-case reliability. Assessment of construct validity in the measurement of clinical reasoning suffers from the difficulty of separating the reasoning process from the underlying knowledge base. As a result, the traditional approach to test validation, namely through correlation with other established methods, is inadequate since it is not clear to what extent these methods measure knowledge and to what extent they assess clinical reasoning [89]. Similarly, inter-case reliability is difficult to achieve because doctors do not perform equally well across all knowledge domains [40], meaning that a large number of cases are required to accurately assess a doctor's fitness to practice.

Assessment Format

Traditionally, clinical reasoning has been informally assessed during ward rounds, practice attachments and the like, and in a more prescribed way, in viva examinations. All these forms of assessment suffer to varying degrees from lack of structure, lack of standardisation, subjective marking, bias in case selection and low inter-rater reliability. In addition, students are tested using only a small and frequently non-representative range of cases that further decrease the reliability and validity of such measures of clinical competence [40]. Moreover, because assessment of clinical competence includes assessment of clinical problem solving, the predominant focus has generally been on examining the end product of the problem-solving process, i.e. diagnosis and treatment. Underlying this approach is the assumption that diagnostic accuracy reflects sound clinical reasoning. In other words, the clinician has worked through the problem in a logical and ordered manner, arriving inevitably at the correct solution. Such an assumption is not always valid, ignoring as it does, other potential influences on the decision-making process such as bias, luck and guess work. This approach also blurs the line separating reasoning ability from problem-solving skill - a factor that needs to be borne in mind throughout this review of methods of assessing clinical reasoning.

Formal assessment of clinical reasoning was not attempted until the early 1960s [172]. Since that time, numerous attempts have been made to develop valid, reliable and practical assessment methods. Because the degree of clinical realism has a direct effect on the validity of the assessment, the vast majority of these methods comprise a clinical scenario containing variable amounts of patient information with specific questions contained within them [173]. The choice of question format is also critical to the validity of the assessment.

- *Multiple Choice Questions (MCQs), Extended Matching Questions (EMQs), long and short menu items*, and other similar formats have the advantage of easy and consistent scoring systems and consequently, high reliability. However, they are more suited to testing factual knowledge and its application than to evaluating a cognitive process such as clinical reasoning. As well, by giving options, they are vulnerable to charges of cueing the student to the answer which in turn, decreases validity [173].
- *Essay Questions* are open-ended and so overcome the problem of cueing. They are suitable for testing knowledge application rather than facts but

are difficult to mark consistently and so tend to have low reliability [174, 175]. As well, essays are time consuming to write which means that, to overcome content specificity and ensure acceptable validity, extended testing time is required since many topics need to be covered.

- *Short Answer Questions* provide a degree of compromise in the dilemma of validity versus reliability posed by these formats. Short answer questions are open-ended, thus overcoming cueing and are able to test a representative range of knowledge in a feasible time period, thereby improving content validity. Although consistent and reliable marking is more difficult to achieve than with MCQs and the like, they do have the capacity to test higher cognitive levels of knowledge [176] and to assess cognitive processes.

There are three broad categories of methods for the specific assessment of clinical reasoning: written response formats, verbal response formats or protocols and computer-based clinical simulations. These methods are now discussed, taking into account the effects of question format on validity and reliability.

Written Formats

The First Generation: Assessing Diagnostic Accuracy

As stated above, formal assessment of clinical reasoning began in the early 1960s with Rimoldi's study of clinical reasoning from the psychometric perspective [172]. This involved presenting students with a problem in the form of a clinical scenario and inviting them to solve it. Additional information could be obtained by choosing questions from a series of cards, each with the corresponding answer on the reverse side. Diagnostic ability was measured by analysing the nature and sequence of the questions "asked". Rimoldi found that experts asked fewer and more focussed questions compared to novices, and concluded that this method could be used both to measure diagnostic skill and to train students in clinical reasoning. His work formed the basis of the subsequent development of the Diagnostic Management Problem [177] and the Patient Management Problem [97].

Patient Management Problems (PMPs) were the method of choice for assessing clinical reasoning throughout the 1960s and 1970s. Unfortunately, their popularity owed more to their relative clinical realism than their psychometric capacity to measure problem-solving skill. The basic procedure involve a staged unfolding of a patient problem plus a list of options about the patient's history, examination and investigations, Students were asked to choose from this list any further data needed, to interpret the data collected and to make diagnostic and management decisions. The student's reasoning path was then compared to that of a reference group, with marks being given for characteristics such as thoroughness, efficiency and accuracy [40].

Although PMPs were seen as having face validity, there are several difficulties with them. Firstly, their question format means they are vulnerable to cueing which can lead to falsely improved scores, thus skewing overall performance [178, 179]. Secondly, there are difficulties with the scoring system. Because PMPs rely on a weighted system of comparison with reference criteria, it is difficult to score them in such a way as to reward competence and efficiency rather than thoroughness of data gathering – a characteristic not related to diagnostic accuracy [180]. The result is that true expert performances, which are characterised by efficient and focussed use of clinical information, are penalised while it is possible for "thorough novices" to achieve falsely high scores [179, 181]. Thirdly, the correlation of scores across PMPs was poor [180] suggesting that case content strongly influences measurement of performance. This finding raised questions about whether PMPs were actually measuring problem-solving skill, or knowledge. Several studies have shown that the problem of content specificity is common to virtually all methods which purport to measure aspects of clinical competence [60, 182, 183], This emphasises the inherent difficulty of devising a way of evaluating the clinical reasoning process that is independent of knowledge.

Several variants of the PMP were developed in an attempt to address these issues, usually by focussing on specific aspects of the diagnostic reasoning process. Such methods include Sequential Management Problems [184], Modified Essay Questions [185] and Simulations of Initial Problem-Solving (SIMPs) [182].

Sequential Management Problems (SMPs) are also founded on the sequential unfolding of a case and begin with a clinical vignette. Based on the information contained, students are asked to identify the additional data required. Their answers are collected and more information provided. Questions are then posed relating to data interpretation, further data required or diagnosis and management.

Modified Essay Questions (MEQs) require students to write short essay-type answers to questions related to specific aspects of each sequentially supplied piece of clinical information.

Both these methods have acceptable reliability provided there are enough of them to overcome content specificity (the alpha coefficient for MEQs approaches 0.9 over a four hour exam [173]) and have face and content validity as measures of clinical competence [186, 187]. Additionally, both feature written responses to open questions rather than allowing the student to choose from a range of options as in PMPs, thus reducing the impact of cueing in individual questions and increasing validity. However, scoring still emphasises content knowledge and diagnostic accuracy rather than the cognitive process of clinical reasoning.

Simulations of Initial Problem-Solving: Although also derived from PMPs, Simulations of Initial Problem-Solving (SIMPs) [182] are different in that they focus on the importance of early hypothesis generation in successful problem solving [12, 56]. SIMPs present a number of clinical scenarios consisting only of the presenting complaint, its history and the contextual features of the case, including the presence of any visible cues, such as a rash or a limp. Using this minimal information, students are asked what they would do to "solve the problem". This method has considerable advantages: its open-ended question format removes the problem of cueing almost entirely; and each scenario can be completed in less than 10 minutes, thus allowing multiple cases to be tested in a reasonable time period and minimising content specificity. Psychometric analysis has shown SIMPS to have acceptable reliability but has been unable to provide firm evidence of construct validity [188] since it is not clear which aspects of clinical skill SIMPs actually measure.

In addition to emphasising the importance of content specificity, and therefore, the role of knowledge and its organisation in clinical expertise [6, 12, 16], the limitations of these methods with regard to validity and reliability, led to increasing concern over the use of the psychometric approach to measuring clinical reasoning ability. Consequently, there was a shift in emphasis from the measurement of problem-solving skill to the characterisation and evaluation of the clinical reasoning process. It was concluded that clinical reasoning has two components – knowledge, and what has been termed "higher order control processes" [189] which include problem-solving strategies such as hypothetico-deductive reasoning and meta-cognition.

The New Generation: Assessing the Process

Key Feature Problems: The 1990s saw the development of methods of assessing clinical reasoning which reflect these conclusions. The first of these, the Key Feature Problems (KFPs), were originally designed to replace the Patient Management Problems which, at the time, formed the basis of the Medical

Council of Canada's Qualifying Examination in Medicine as a measure of clinical decision-making skill [190-192]. KFPs are based on the concept that every clinical problem contains certain critical elements, or key features, essential to its resolution. These are unique to each case, and may occur at different stages of the diagnostic process. Each KFP consists of a short clinical scenario with a limited amount of information and asks questions that rely on the candidate successfully identifying and interpreting the case's key features, and that test for the procedural knowledge needed to reach the correct diagnosis. Questions may be open-ended requiring a short written response or they may be presented as a stem with a menu of options (up to 45 items) from which to choose. While these formats do not completely eradicate cueing, they minimise it, thereby decreasing the chance of obtaining falsely high scores and increasing overall accuracy. Each problem can be completed in a relatively short period of time (approximately five minutes), thus enabling many different problems to be tested over the period of the examination (three to three and a half hours). Although construct validity has not been analysed, KFPs have demonstrated face and content validity, and acceptable reliability (alpha coefficient = 0.80) if presented as a set of 40 problems. As well, by focussing exclusively on the key features of a case, efficiency and effectiveness, rather than thoroughness of data-gathering, are rewarded. However, KFPs are essentially still another method for measuring the outcomes of clinical competence rather than directly evaluating aspects of the reasoning process.

Clinical Reasoning Exercises (CREs) were developed specifically as an assessment instrument for PBL curricula, and are designed to test either pathophysiological knowledge or hypothesis generation [193, 194]. Each consists of a short clinical scenario followed by a single open-ended question. Students are asked either for a pathophysiological explanation of the information provided or to formulate hypotheses to explain the clinical features of the case and to suggest the most likely diagnosis. When presented as a set of 15 exercises, taking about 1.5 hours to complete and used to test knowledge, the CREs have acceptable reliability (alpha coefficient = 0.78) and modest correlation with knowledge (r = 0.46). When used to measure clinical reasoning, CREs are slightly less reliable, possibly a consequence of using fewer exercises per test (alpha coefficient = 0.69 over eight exercises). A disattenuated correlation coefficient (r) of 0.62 with a test for clinical competence (Objective Structured Clinical Examination) indicates that while this type of CRE measures elements of both knowledge and performance, its validity as a measure of clinical reasoning remains to be assessed.

While KFPs and other recently developed techniques, such as the CREs, have been able to minimise the effects of cueing and content specificity, no single technique has emerged which is completely satisfactory in its ability to validly and reliably assess either clinical problem-solving skill or the clinical reasoning process. More importantly, none even profess to evaluate the clinical reasoning process other than indirectly and implicitly. The Script Concordance Test was developed in an attempt to tackle these shortcomings.

The Script Concordance Test (SCT) [195] is based on the script theory of the development of clinical expertise [7, 8, 87] and is designed to assess the extent of knowledge organisation by measuring the level of script development. The SCT assesses the diagnostic, investigative or therapeutic knowledge of the subject and consists of short clinical scenarios, each containing all the relevant clinical information needed to respond to sets of test items. Each item posits several diagnostic hypotheses and aims to determine the effect of further information on those hypotheses based on comparison with expert performance. Items are scored using a five-point Likert-type scale, a scoring system that prevents cueing. The scoring system also recognises that an important consequence of the idiosyncratic nature of expert clinical reasoning is that there are a number of different but correct reasoning paths and takes account of this by using an aggregate scoring method instead of the more usual consensus method [196, 197]. Thus, the SCT focuses on the interpretation of clinical information as part of the clinical reasoning process. It is easily administered with a consistent and straightforward scoring system, and has acceptable reliability (alpha coefficient = 0.80 for a test consisting of about 50 scenarios). Scores on the SCT have been shown to increase with clinical experience, indicating not only that it discriminates between levels of expertise but has construct validity. As with all methods though, the SCT does have limitations. The length of time required for satisfactory reliability is not given, but it can be surmised that if each scenario takes five minutes to complete, a testing time in excess of four hours would be required - which is at the upper limit of feasibility for students and examiners alike. Furthermore, by assessing a single aspect of diagnosis, namely interpretation of clinical information, it provides a less comprehensive picture of the clinical reasoning process than would be obtained if identification of key features and hypothesis generation were also examined. Nevertheless, the SCT provides the most direct and realistic assessment of the written response methods reviewed so far.

Clinical Reasoning Problems (CRPs) [198] was developed as a research method to measure and describe clinical reasoning in undergraduate medical students. It consists of a clinical scenario comprising patient presentation, history and physical examination. Based on this information, students are required to decide on the most likely diagnosis, to list and indicate the relative importance of, the clinical features they identified as being relevant to that diagnosis. The scoring scheme is designed to assess the reasoning process rather than diagnostic accuracy and to reward discrimination, rather than thoroughness, in data collection. Presented as a set of ten problems, the CRPs have been shown to be reliable, valid and practicable for use with large numbers of students. By concentrating on the first three steps in the clinical reasoning process – identification and interpretation of clinical data and hypothesis generation – the CRPs are able to provide a more comprehensive depiction of an individual's clinical reasoning.

While the CRPs have been shown to overcome many of the problems that bedevil other written formats, the qualitative nature and complexity of its scoring scheme makes it time-consuming and labour-intensive. Although suitable for use with individual students for teaching purposes, this limits its routine use for large-scale assessment.

It will be observed that the methods described above employ some form of clinical simulation as their context. However, there have been attempts to develop methods that are not necessarily based in a clinical environment, that more directly measure and evaluate the cognitive processes which occur as a clinician works through a problem. Examples of this approach are the Medical Reasoning Aptitude Test (MRAT) [199] and the Diagnostic Thinking Inventory [200]. Although the MRAT assesses generic aspects of the reasoning process such as the quality of hypothesis generation and evaluation, it is designed to be used in conjunction with admission criteria such as GPA, to improve prediction of performance at the level of admission to American medical schools. Consequently, it will not be considered further.

The Diagnostic Thinking Inventory: The primary objective of the Diagnostic Thinking Inventory (DTI) [200] is to provide insight into the clinical reasoning process. It is therefore applicable to the assessment of clinical reasoning at all levels of expertise. Specifically, it is designed to evaluate reasoning style and attitudes and assumes that skill in diagnosis is related to these characteristics. A major advantage of this instrument is that it is truly independent of knowledge. Thus, it is able to provide direct insight into the nature of the subject's clinical reasoning process.

The DTI is a self-evaluation questionnaire of 41 items, each intended to assess one of two aspects of diagnostic thinking - flexibility of thinking or knowledge organisation. All items consist of two opposing statements separated by a six-point semantic scale representing a continuum between the two statements. Students are asked to indicate where on the scale, their position lies with regard to their diagnostic thinking. The DTI has been shown to have acceptable reliability (alpha coefficient > 0.80) as well as the ability to discriminate between levels of expertise [201-203].

Although the DTI has demonstrable face and content validity for the evaluation of clinical reasoning style [200-203], arguments for construct validity are based on the premise that experts have greater diagnostic thinking ability than do novices and that this is reflected in the scores obtained [203]. However, the DTI's scoring system is based on the assumption of a relationship between a particular style of clinical reasoning (or diagnostic thinking) and diagnostic skill, which contradicts evidence of the idiosyncratic nature of expert reasoning [8, 71, 120]. As a consequence, claims that the DTI has construct validity are questionable. Furthermore, as with all forms of self-evaluation, results are susceptible to bias due to the temptation for subjects to respond in ways they perceive as being "right" or more acceptable rather than in ways which are a true reflection of how they actually think. Although these shortcomings limit the usefulness of the DTI in studies investigating clinical reasoning, it has nevertheless been used successfully by its developers to identify strengths and weaknesses in individual students, and by others to relate the development of clinical reasoning to learning styles and knowledge [202] and to measure the effects of specific educational interventions [201, 204].

Overall, written response formats have several advantages with regard to their practical application. They are easily administered to large samples. They are able to test a wide range of medical knowledge, have reasonable clinical fidelity and are relatively easy to score, especially if objectively formatted questions are used. However, these very advantages also cause some problems. Firstly, the use of objectively formatted questions (such as Multiple True/False, Extended Matching Questions and Multiple Choice Questions) frequently cues the student to the correct answer. They are also more suited to testing knowledge content than evaluating the reasoning process. On the other hand, open question formats are susceptible to rater bias and require a marking scheme based on criterion referencing. This, in turn, leads to problems of validation and standardisation [200]. Secondly, with the exception of the DTI, these methods tend to concentrate on specific aspects of diagnosis rather than on the clinical reasoning process as a whole. Thirdly, and most importantly (and with few exceptions), assessment of the clinical reasoning process is implicit rather than direct. Verbal response formats attempt to correct this aspect.

Verbal Response Formats

Verbal response formats are based on the premise that the most accurate way of evaluating the reasoning used in the diagnostic process is by direct access to the clinician's thoughts as s/he works through a clinical problem. This premise was initially explored in cognitive psychology research into reasoning and decision-making [88, 205] and was first applied to medicine in the 1970s [12], marking a more qualitative approach to the study of clinical reasoning.

Verbal response formats present students with a clinical case, either as a "live" simulation using standardized patients or as a written scenario, and asks them to verbalise their thinking. The resulting protocols are recorded and evaluated using either semantic or propositional analysis. There are several forms of verbal response which are used to study different aspects of the clinical reasoning process. These can be broadly categorised as either simultaneous or retrospective depending on whether the subject verbalises his thinking during or after the "patient encounter", and are referred to variously as "think-aloud" protocols, stimulated recall protocols and explanation protocols [206].

Think-Aloud Protocols

These involve the presentation of a case containing varying amounts of information about the patient's presentation, history, physical examination and investigations. The subject is asked to think aloud as he works through the case to a diagnosis, and to report his thoughts without any theorising about the cognitive processes that are producing them. The objectives of think-aloud research are to identify the clinical features used to decide on the diagnosis (and so is partly a measure of knowledge); and to gain insight into the reasoning process. That is, to discover how knowledge is used and how the interrelationships between concepts are established that enables the diagnosis to be made. It has been used extensively in research on expert-novice differences [207], particularly into the use of contextual information [148] and the way the problem is represented in the clinician's mind [208, 209].

Stimulated Recall Protocols

Stimulated recall protocols have also been used in the investigation of expert-novice differences [210], as well as by Elstein and colleagues in their work on medical problem-solving [12]. Stimulated recall differs from the think-aloud method in that the subject's verbalisations are recorded after diagnosis and management decisions have been made. The implication is that such protocols contain material which has been "filtered" by the subject and therefore, represents a mixture of recall of case detail, comprehension statements, metacognitive activity and application of knowledge [206]. Stimulated recall methodology has shown that the nature and amount of clinical information recalled varies with level of expertise [66, 210], level of knowledge organisation and available time [66], with case difficulty [71] and with early hypothesis generation [56].

Explanation Protocols

These are another form of retrospective verbal response, but differ from stimulated recall in that the subject is asked to provide a pathophysiological explanation of the clinical features of the case. Much of the research on the integration of biomedical and clinical science knowledge has been performed using this type of verbal response [127]. Explanation protocols have provided insights into the relationship of reasoning type with level of expertise [13]. Additionally, this method has been used extensively to investigate the intermediate effect in the development of expertise [65].

Protocol Analysis

Protocols obtained by verbal response methodology can be examined in two ways, propositional analysis or semantic analysis:

Propositional analysis [13] is based on the notion that verbal response protocols contain "chunks" of knowledge, or propositions, which are related to each other by links. These links have direction and can be either causal or conditional in nature. The result is a network of concepts (represented as nodes) connected by relations (or links) which indicate both the direction of reasoning (forward or backward) and the nature of the connection between propositions or concepts [206].

Semantic analysis [141] employs the same principle but contends that both syntax and semantics play a major role in describing the relationship between "chunks" of knowledge. Syntax defines the diagnostic entity (e.g. hypoxia) to which a sign or symptom belongs and determines whether it precedes or follows a diagnostic interpretation. Semantics defines the meaning given to the sign or symptom and allows that meaning to be abstracted and associated via semantic axes with other abstractions, thereby forming networks of semantic qualities in the clinician's memory. A corollary of this model is that the meaning of a sign/symptom can only be fully understood in relation to other signs/symptoms present in the patient [114].

Verbal response formats have intuitive appeal because they utilise a "stream of consciousness" approach that ideally, provides direct access to the clinical reasoning process. However, they have been criticised on three grounds. Firstly, a great deal of cognitive processing occurs at the sub-conscious level; secondly, subjects may be inclined to say what they think the researcher wants to hear, rather than providing a verbatim report of their thought processes [211]; and thirdly, there is potential for confusing expertise and self-confidence with reasoning [212]. Consequently, verbal protocols may not be an accurate reflection of the reasoning process. As well, they are impracticable for use with large numbers of subjects because of the length of time required for representative testing of knowledge and the complexity and laboriousness of protocol analysis which requires knowledge of semantics and is difficult to standardise. That is, they are effectively limited to experimental purposes.

Computer Based Simulations

Computer based clinical simulations do not so much provide another approach as provide a considerably more flexible and efficient instrument for assessing both reasoning and knowledge [213]. Over the past 10-20 years, their use has become increasingly widespread and popular especially in PBL curricula where explicit and formal tuition in clinical reasoning is a major focus. There are many types of program, some designed for general assessment [214, 215] and some to assess different aspects of student learning, including early hypothesis generation [216], clinical decision-making through identification of key features [217] and the effects of integrated problem-based learning curricula [218]. The common requirement is that students work through a clinical case by collecting a history, "performing" a physical exam, ordering and interpreting laboratory tests and other investigations, and prescribing treatment. The emphasis throughout is on the investigative process used rather than diagnostic accuracy. The student's enquiry strategy is assessed and analysed against certain criteria characteristic of expert problem solvers, thus providing a measure of clinical reasoning. Computerised clinical simulations for both educational and assessment purposes have several advantages over the other previously described formats:

Clinical Reality: The potential for interaction between the subject, as the doctor, and the computer, as the patient, means that the clinical reality that can be achieved is appreciably greater than with paper cases. Real-life situations are frequently characterised by lack of structure, poorly presented patient information in which it is often difficult to separate the relevant from the extraneous, and data gathering which is available spasmodically over time rather than being presented in one neat package at the outset. Not only are computerised simulations better at simulating clinical reality, they are also able to incorporate both static and moving images so that visual cues and the results of medical imaging investigations, such as ultrasonography, become part of the available information.

Scoring: The complex analysis required to evaluate the large amount of data obtained is incorporated into the program, thus ensuring fast, standardised and reliable scoring.

Flexibility: Most programs provide the opportunity for customisation so that both cases and analysis can be modified to suit the needs of individual institution's curricula or of individual students, thereby providing a degree of flexibility unattainable with other methods. Included in this is the capacity to alter not only the structure and content of the patient encounter itself but the type of information required and the form in which that information is sought [219]. That is, computer based simulations can present single or multiple patient encounters, varying levels of volunteered patient information, interpreted or un-interpreted clinical findings, and a diverse range of question format (open-ended, multiple choice, extended matching or short-answer) depending on whether assessment of knowledge or of the reasoning process is the main objective. They can also provide users with feedback about their progress through the case in various ways.

However, computer-based simulations have some drawbacks, particularly in regard to research into clinical reasoning using large sample sizes. Firstly, they are complex to use, requiring subjects to be pre-trained before testing. Secondly, although theoretically they are applicable to large numbers of students because data analysis is part of the program, in practice, administering them to large numbers of geographically dispersed students may be logistically difficult, due to the requirement for multiple copies of the software to be available at easily accessible locations. While this may be less of a problem if the objective is solely educational, it becomes more so if assessment is the primary purpose. Consequently, they are effectively only useful for qualitative research using small numbers of selected students.

Chapter 6

Implications for Medical Education

The difficulty of characterising the clinical reasoning process, the idiosyncratic nature of expert clinical reasoning and the difficulty of assessing clinical reasoning skill has lead some to speculate on whether clinical reasoning can be formally taught or whether it can only be learned through experience [220]. However, other work suggests that there are specific aspects of the clinical reasoning process that are not reliant solely on experience and can be usefully taught to medical students – aspects such as the early exploration of relevant diagnostic hypotheses and the collection of relevant clinical data [46]. Similarly, the use of pathophysiology by experts to create coherence in their diagnostic explanations [221] vindicates the importance of teaching basic science knowledge.

While there are many studies which advocate teaching of various clinical reasoning strategies, including specific types of knowledge representation, schema, algorithms and disease patterns [222-224], a major factor in successful teaching clinical reasoning ability is associated with the difficulty of recognising and applying relevant knowledge learned in a situation to other similar situations, i.e. analogic transfer [98]. To facilitate transfer, two approaches appear effective – the use of multiple examples when teaching clinical reasoning [224] and deliberate practice. As Norman suggests, "focussing instruction on one processing strategy or another may be less important than engaging students with many problems which are carefully sequenced to optimise learning and transfer" [10]

When it comes to the assessment of clinical reasoning, it is clear that, despite numerous attempts and increasing understanding of the clinical reasoning process, there is still no gold standard when it comes to its assessment and evaluation. The choice of method can be made only after careful consideration of the purpose of the assessment, the particular circumstances in which it is to be conducted and established criteria. It is important to realise that the most direct methods, such as verbal response formats, although possibly more valid measures of clinical reasoning, are expensive, time consuming, labour-intensive and entail complex analysis procedures which make them impracticable for assessing large numbers of subjects where reliability and feasibility are also of major concern. Any technique for large scale assessment of clinical reasoning should meet the following basic criteria:

- Be able to test across a range of systems and pathological processes to eliminate content specificity;
- Feature problems that are clinically realistic;
- Employ non-directional questions to allow maximum freedom of response and minimise cueing;
- Be easily administered;
- Be able to be completed within a practicable time frame;
- Have a scoring scheme that is unambiguous, consistent, reliable and sensitive to differences between levels of expertise.

The development and implementation of valid, reliable and feasible methods for evaluating clinical reasoning has become even more pressing since the widespread introduction of integrated, problem-based learning (PBL) curricula in medical schools. In contrast to conventional, didactic, discipline-based courses, in which acquisition of clinical reasoning expertise tends to be haphazard and heavily dependent on the nature of the clinical experience and the quality of supervision, PBL places formal emphasis on the teaching and development of clinical reasoning as well as problem-solving skills. There is, therefore, a concomitant need for its formal assessment. Further, the method of assessment needs to reflect the method of learning [225]. Thus, while written formats and computer-based simulations may be appropriate for the early years of undergraduate medical training, in the so-called "clinical years" when students are in full-time hospital attachments, and for postgraduate training, the use of clinical examinations using standardised patients becomes increasingly necessary to test candidates' ability to integrate their knowledge with all the individual patient factors (clinical, contextual, social) that must be considered and applied in order to make correct diagnostic and management decisions.

Conclusion

The central role of experiential knowledge in the development of diagnostic expertise has been repeatedly demonstrated and acknowledged throughout this review. The challenge for medical educators at both the undergraduate and postgraduate level is to attempt to accelerate this process in their teaching via appropriate learning strategies, the provision of continuous opportunities for deliberate practice and by ensuring that assessment reflects both knowledge content and its method of acquisition as well as the level of competence required for practice [224, 226]. It is in this way that medical schools can meet their responsibility to the medical profession and the community at large to graduate students able to diagnose and manage patients correctly and effectively, thereby contribute to the reduction of adverse events through diagnostic error and increased patient safety.

References

[1]   Andrews LB, Stocking C, Krizek T, Gottlieb L, Krizek C, Vargish T, et al.
      An alternative strategy for studying adverse events in medical care. *Lancet.*
      1997 Feb 1; 349(9048):309-13.

[2]   Leape LL, Brennan TA, Laird N, Lawthers AG, Localio AR, Barnes BA, et
      al. The nature of adverse events in hospitalized patients. Results of the
      Harvard Medical Practice Study II. *The New England journal of medicine.*
      1991 Feb 7; 324(6):377-84.

[3]   Thomas E, Studdert D, Burstin H, al. e. Incidence and types of adverse
      events and negligent care in Utah and Colorado. *Medical Care.* 2000;
      38:261-2.

[4]   Wilson RM, Runciman WB, Gibberd RW, Harrison BT, Newby L,
      Hamilton JD. The Quality in Australian Health Care Study. *Med. J. Aust.*
      1995; 163(9):458-71.

[5]   Wilson R, Harrison B, Gibberd R, Hamilton J. An analysis of the cause of
      adverse events from the Quality in Australian Health Care Study. *Med. J.
      Aust.* 1999; 170:411-5.

[6]   Bordage G, Zacks R. The structure of medical knowledge in the memories
      of medical students and general practitioners: categories and prototypes.
      Med. Educ. 1984; 18(6):406-16.

[7]   Feltovich P, Barrows H. Issues of generality in medical problem solving. In:
      Schmidt H, de Volder M, eds. *Tutorials in Problem-Based Learning: A New
      Direction in Teaching the Health Professions.* Assen, The Netherlands: Van
      Gorcum 1984:128-42.

[8]   Schmidt HG, Norman GR, Boshuizen HP. A cognitive perspective on
      medical expertise: theory and implications. *Acad. Med.* 1990; 65(10):611-
      21.

[9]   Grant R. Obsolescence or lifelong education: choices and challenges. *Physiotherapy.* 1992; 78:167-71.

[10]   Norman G. Research in clinical reasoning: past history and current trends. *Med. Educ.* 2005 Apr; 39(4):418-27.

[11]   Barrows H, Feightner J, Neufeld V, Norman G. *An Analysis of the Clinical Methods of Medical Students and Physicians.* Hamilton, Ontario: Province of Ontarion Department of Health, McMaster University; 1978.

[12]   Elstein A, Shulman L, Sprafka S. *Medical Problem Solving: An Analysis of Clinical Reasoning.* Cambridge, MA: Harvard University Press; 1978.

[13]   Patel VL, Groen GJ. Knowledge-based solution strategies in medical reasoning. *Cog. Sci.* 1986; 10:91-116.

[14]   Kassirer J, Kopelman R. *Learning Clinical Reasoning.* Baltimore: Williams and Wilkins; 1991.

[15]   Feinstein A. An analysis of diagnostic reasoning. 1. The domains and disorders of clinical macrobiology. *Yale J. Biol. Med.* 1973; 46:212-32.

[16]   Barrows H, Feltovich P. The clinical reasoning process. *Med. Educ.* 1987; 21(2):86-91.

[17]   Arocha JF, Patel VL, Patel YC. Hypothesis generation and the coordination of theory and evidence in novice diagnostic reasoning. *Med. Decis. Making.* 1993; 13(3):198-211.

[18]   Kassirer JP. Diagnostic Reasoning. *Annals of Internal Medicine.* 1989; 110:893-900.

[19]   Pauker SG, Kassirer JP. Therapeutic decision making: a cost-benefit analysis. *The New England journal of medicine.* 1975; 293(5):229-34.

[20]   Pauker SG, Kassirer JP. The threshold approach to clinical decision making. *The New England journal of medicine.* 1980; 302(20):1109-17.

[21]   Sox HC, Jr. Probability theory in the use of diagnostic tests. An introduction to critical study of the literature. *Ann. Intern. Med.* 1986; 104(1):60-6.

[22]   Newell A, Simon HA. Human *Problem Solving.* Englewood Cliffs, New Jersey: Prentice-Hall; 1972.

[23]   Tversky A, Kahneman D. Judgement under uncertainty: heuristics and biases. *Science.* 1974; 185:1124-31.

[24]   Kahneman D, Slovic P, Tversky A. *Judgement under Uncertainty: Heuristics and Biases.* Cambridge: Cambridge University Press; 1982.

[25]   Stillings N, Feinstein M, Garfield J, al e. *Cognitive Science: An Introduction.* Cambridge: MIT Press; 1987.

[26] Langley P, Simon H, Bradshaw G, Zytkow J. *Scientific Discovery: Computational Explorations of the Creative Process.* Cambridge, MA: MIT Press; 1987.

[27] Kassirer JP, Gorry GA. Clinical problem solving: a behavioral analysis. *Ann. Intern. Med.* 1978; 89(2):245-55.

[28] Newell A. Artificial intelligence and the concept of mind. In: Shank R, Colby K, eds. *Computer Models of Thought and Language.* San Francisco: WH Freeman; 1973:1-60.

[29] Holland J, Holyoak K, Nisbett R, Thagard P. *Induction: Processes of Inference, Learning and Discovery.* Cambridge.MA: MIT Press 1986.

[30] Kassirer JP, Kopelman RI. Judging causality. *Hosp. Pract.* (Off Ed). 1987; 22(10):43-6, 8, 50.

[31] Barrows H, Bennett K. The diagnostic (problem solving) skill of the neurologist. Experimental studies and their implications for neurological training. *Arch Neurol.* 1972; 26(3):273-7.

[32] Barrows HS, Tamblyn RM. *Problem-Based Learning: An Approach to Medical Education.* New York: Springer Publishing Co. 1980.

[33] Bergus GR, Chapman GB, Gjerde C, Elstein AS. Clinical reasoning about new symptoms despite preexisting disease: sources of error and order effects. *Fam. Med.* 1995 May; 27(5):314-20.

[34] Scott I. Understanding and developing clinical reasoning skills: Australian and New Zealand Association of Medical Education, 1996.

[35] Custers EJ, Stuyt PM, De Vries Robbe PF. Clinical problem analysis (CPA): a systematic approach to teaching complex medical problem solving. *Acad. Med.* 2000; 75(3):291-7.

[36] Woloschuk W, Harasym P, Mandin H, Jones A. Use of scheme-based problem solving: an evaluation of the implementation and utilization of schemes in a clinical presentation curriculum. *Med. Educ.* 2000; 34(6):437-42.

[37] Barrows H, Pickell G. *Developing Clinical Problem Solving Skills: A Guide to More Effective Diagnosis and Treatment.* New York: Norton and Comp; 1991.

[38] Groen GJ, Patel VL. Medical problem-solving: some questionable assumptions. *Med. Educ.* 1985; 19(2):95-100.

[39] Elstein A, Shulman L, Sprafka S. Medical problem solving: a ten year retrospective. *Evaluation and the Health Professions.* 1990; 13:5-36.

[40] Van der Vleuten CP, Newble DI. How can we test clinical reasoning? *Lancet* 1995; 345:1032-4.

[41] Norman GR, Coblentz CL, Brooks LR, Babcook CJ. Expertise in visual diagnosis: a review of the literature. *Acad. Med.* 1992; 67(10 Suppl):S78-83.

[42] Gale J, Marsden P. Clinical problem solving: the beginning of the process. *Med. Educ.* 1982; 16(1):22-6.

[43] Patel VL, Groen GJ. Developmental accounts of the transition from medical student to doctor: some problems and suggestions. *Med. Educ.* 1991; 25(6):527-35.

[44] Patel V, Arocha J, Groen G. Strategy selection and degree of expertise in medical reasoning. 8th *Cognitive Science Society Annual Conference;* 1986; 1986.

[45] Rikers RM, Schmidt HG, Boshuizen HP, Linssen GC, Wesseling G, Paas FG. The robustness of medical expertise: clinical case processing by medical experts and subexperts. *Am. J. Psychol.* 2002 Winter; 115(4):609-29.

[46] Nendaz MR, Gut AM, Perrier A, Louis-Simonet M, Blondon-Choa K, Herrmann FR, et al. Brief report: beyond clinical experience: features of data collection and interpretation that contribute to diagnostic accuracy. *J. Gen. Intern. Med.* 2006 Dec; 21(12):1302-5.

[47] Perkins D, Salomon G. Are cognitive skills context bound? *Educ. Res.* 1989; 18:16-25.

[48] Patel VL, Groen GJ, Arocha JF. Medical expertise as a function of task difficulty. *Mem. Cognit.* 1990; 18(4):394-406.

[49] Bordage G, Lemieux M. Some cognitive characteristics of medical students with and without diagnostic reasoning difficulties. 25th *Annual Conference of Research in Medical Education of the American Association of Medical Colleges;* 1987; New Orleans, Louisiana: American Association of Medical Colleges; 1987. p. 185-90.

[50] Grant J, Marsden P. The structure of memorized knowledge in students and clinicians: an explanation for diagnostic expertise. *Med. Educ.* 1987; 21(2):92-8.

[51] Hassebrock F, Jonas A, Bauer L. Metacognitive aspects of medical problem solving. *Annual Meeting of the American Educational Research Association;* 1993; Atlanta, GA: American Educational Research Association; 1993.

[52] Higgs J, Jones M. Clinical Reasoning. In: Higgs J, Jones M, eds. *Clinical Reasoning in the Health Professions.* Oxford; Boston: Butterworth-Heinemann 1995:3-23.

[53] Elstein AS. Clinical Reasoning in Medicine. In: Higgs J, Jones M, eds. *Clinical Reasoning in the Health Professions.* Oxford; Boston: Butterworth - Heinemann 1995:49-59.

[54] Eddy DM, Clanton CH. The art of diagnosis: solving the clinicopathological exercise. *The New England journal of medicine.* 1982; 306(21):1263-8.

[55] Elstein A. What goes around comes around: the return of the hypothetico-deductive strategy. *Teaching and Learning in Medicine.* 1994; 6:121-3.

[56] Barrows H, Norman G, Neufeld V, Feightner J. The clinical reasoning of randomly selected physicians in general medical practice. *Clin. Invest Med.* 1982; 5(1):49-55.

[57] Neufeld VR, Norman GR, Feightner JW, Barrows HS. Clinical problem-solving by medical students: a cross-sectional and longitudinal analysis. *Med. Educ.* 1981; 15(5):315-22.

[58] Norman GR, Tugwell P, Feightner JW, Muzzin LJ, Jacoby LL. Knowledge and clinical problem-solving. *Med. Educ.* 1985; 19(5):344-56.

[59] Norcini J, Swanson D, Gross L, Webster G. A comparison of several methods for scoring patient management problems. *Research in Medical Education;* 1983; Washington, DC; 1983.

[60] Swanson D, Norcini J, Grosso L. Assessment of clinical competence: Written and computer-based simulations. *Assess Eval Higher Educ.* 1987; 12:220-46.

[61] Norman G, Tugwell R, Feightner J. A comparison of resident performance on real and simulated patients. *J. Med. Educ.* 1982; 57:708-15.

[62] Maatsch J, Munger B, Podgorny G. Reliability and validity of the Board examination in emergency medicine. *Emergency Medicine Annual 1.* Norwalk: Appleton, Century, Croft; 1982.

[63] Maatsch J, Huang R. An evaluation of the construct validity of four alternative theories of clinical competence. *Annual Conference of Research into Medical Education;* 1986; 1986. p. 69-74.

[64] Grant J, Marsden P. Primary knowledge, medical education and consultant expertise. *Med. Educ.* 1988; 22:746-53.

[65] Schmidt H, Boshuizen H, Hobus P. Transitory stages in the development of medical expertise: The "intermediate effect" in clinical case presentation studies. *The Tenth Annual Conference of the Cognitive Science Society;* 1988; Montreal, Quebec, Canada; 1988. p. 139-45.

[66] Schmidt HG, Boshuizen HP. On the origin of intermediate effects in clinical case recall. *Mem. Cognit.* 1993; 21(3):338-51.

[67] Norman GR, Patel VL, Schmidt HG. Clinical inquiry and scientific inquiry. *Med. Educ.* 1990; 24(4):396-9.

[68] Schmidt H, de Grave W, de Volder M, Moust J, Patel V. Explanatory models in the processing of science text: the role of prior knowledge activation through small-group discussion. *J. Educ. Psychol.* 1989; 81:481-91.

[69] Barnett R. *The Idea of Higher Education.* Buckingham: The Society for Research into Higher Education and Open University Press; 1990.

[70] Schon D. *Educating the Reflective Practitioner.* San Francisco: Jossey-Bass; 1987.

[71] Norman G, Brooks L, Allen S. Recall by expert medical practitioners and novices as a record of processing attention. *J Experimental Psychology: Learning, Memory and Cognition.* 1989; 13:1116-74.

[72] Weber E, Bockenholt U, Hilton D, Wallace B. Determinants of diagnostic hypothesis generation: effects of information, base rates and experience. *J. Exp. Psychol. Learn Mem. Cogn.* 1993; 19:1151-64.

[73] Cutler P. *Problem Solving in Clinical Medicine: From Data to Diagnosis.* Baltimore: Williams and Wilkins; 1979.

[74] Lemieux M, Bordage G. Propositional versus structural semantic analyses of medical diagnostic thinking. *Cog. Sci.* 1992; 16:185-204.

[75] Custers EJ, Regehr G, Norman GR. Mental representations of medical diagnostic knowledge: a review. *Acad. Med.* 1996; 71(10 Suppl):S55-61.

[76] Smith E, Medin D. *Categories and Concepts.* Cambridge, MA: Harvard University Press; 1981.

[77] Neiser U. Nested structure in autobiographical memory. In: Rubin D, ed. *Autobiographical Memory.* Cambridge, UK: Cambridge University Press; 1986.

[78] Nosofsky R. Exemplar-based accounts of relations between classification, recognition and typicality. *J. Exp. Psychol. Learn Mem. Cogn.* 1988; 14(4): 700-8.

[79] Klayman J, Brown K. Debias the environment instead of the judge: an alternative approach to reducing error in diagnostic (and other) judgment. *Cognition.* 1993; 49(1-2):97-122.

[80] Genero N, Cantor N. Exemplar prototypes and clinical diagnosis: toward a cognitive economy. *J. Soc. Clin. Psychol.* 1987; 5(1):59-78.

[81] Brooks L, Norman G, Allen S. Role of specific similarity in a medical diagnostic task. *J. Exp. Psychol. Gen.* 1991; 120(3):278-87.

[82] Allen S, Brooks L. Specializing the operation of an explicit rule. *J. Exp. Psychol. Gen.* 1991; 120(1):3-19.

[83] Read S. Once is enough: reasoning from a single instance. *J. Pers. Soc. Psychol.* 1983; 45(2):323-34.

[84] Allen S, Norman G, Brooks L. Experimental studies of learning dermatological diagnoses: the impact of examples. *Teach Learn Med.* 1992; 4:35-44.

[85] Regehr G, Brooks L. Perceptual manifestations of an analytic structure: the priority of holistic individuation. *J. Exp. Psychol. Gen.* 1993; 122:92-114.

[86] Boshuizen H, Schmidt H. On the role of biomedical knowledge in clinical reasoning by experts, intermediates and novices. *Cog. Sci.* 1992; 16:153-84.

[87] Charlin B, Tardif J, Boshuizen HP. Scripts and medical diagnostic knowledge: theory and applications for clinical reasoning instruction and research. *Acad. Med.* 2000; 75(2):182-90.

[88] Chase W, Simon H. Perception in chess. *Cognitive Psychology.* 1973; 4:55-81.

[89] Schuwirth LW, Verheggen MM, Van Der Vleuten CP, Boshuizen HP, Dinant GJ. Do short cases elicit different thinking processes than factual knowledge questions do? *Med. Educ.* 2001; 35(4):348-56.

[90] Schank R, Abelson R. *Scripts, Plans, Goals and Understanding: An Inquiry into Human Knowledge Structures.* Hillsdale, NJ: Lawrence Erlbaum Associates; 1977.

[91] McGaghie WC, Boerger RL, McCrimmon DR, Ravitch MM. Agreement among medical experts about the structure of concepts in pulmonary physiology. *Acad. Med.* 1994; 69(10 Suppl):S78-80.

[92] Regehr G, Norman GR. Issues in cognitive psychology: implications for professional education. *Acad. Med.* 1996; 71(9):988-1001.

[93] Norman G, Trott A, Brooks L, Smith E. Cognitive differences in clinical reasoning related to postgraduate training. *Teaching and Learning in Medicine.* 1994; 6:114-20.

[94] Guest CB, Regehr G, Tiberius RG. The life long challenge of expertise. *Med. Educ.* 2001; 35(1):78-81.

[95] Smith J, Ericsson K. *Towards a general theory of expertise: prospects and limits.* Cambridge, New York: Cambridge University Press; 1991.

[96] Glaser R, Chi M. Overview. In: Chi M, Glaser, R and Farr, MJ, ed. *The Nature of Expertise.* Hillsdale, New Jersey: Lawrence Erlbaum Associates 1988:xvi-xxviii.

[97] McGuire C, Babbott D. Simulation technique in the measurement of problem-solving skills. *J. Educ. Measur.* 1967; 4:1-10.

[98] Eva KW, Neville AJ, Norman GR. Exploring the etiology of content specificity: factors influencing analogic transfer and problem solving. *Acad. Med.* 1998; 73(10 Suppl):S1-5.

[99] Berner ES, Bligh TJ, Guerin RO. An indication for a process dimension in medical problem-solving. *Med. Educ.* 1977; 11(5):324-8.

[100] Donnely M, Fleischer D, Schvenker J, Chen C. Problem solving within a limited content area. 21st *Conference on Research in Medical Education;* 1982; Washington, DC; 1982.

[101] Skakun E, Taylor W, Wilson D, Taylor T, Grace M, Fincham S. Preliminary investigation of computerised patient management problems in relation to other examinations. *Educational and Psychological Measurement.* 1979; 39:303-10.

[102] Needham DR, Begg IM. Problem-oriented training promotes spontaneous analogical transfer: memory-oriented training promotes memory for training. *Mem. Cognit.* 1991; 19(6):543-57.

[103] Reeves L, Weisberg R. The role of content and abstract information in analogical transfer. *Psychol. Bull.* 1994; 115:381-400.

[104] Gentner D, Toupin C. Systematicity and surface similarity in the development of analogy. *Cogn. Sci.* 1986; 10:277-300.

[105] American BoIM. Clinical competence in internal medicine. *Ann. Intern. Med.* 1979; 90:402-11.

[106] Holyoak K. Mental models in problem solving. In: Anderson J, Kosslyn M, eds. *Tutorials in Learning and Memory.* San Francisco, CA: Freeman; 1984.

[107] Medin D, Ross B. The specific character of abstract thought: categorisation, problem solving and induction. In: Sternberg R, ed. *Advances in the Psychology of Human Intelligence.* Hillsdale, NJ: Erlbaum 1989.

[108] Holyoak KJ, Koh K. Surface and structural similarity in analogical transfer. *Mem. Cognit.* 1987; 15(4):332-40.

[109] Gentner D. Structure mapping: a theoretical framework for analogy. *Cogn. Sci.* 1989; 59:47-59.

[110] Chi M, Feltovich P, Glaser R. Categorisation and representation of physics problems by experts and novices. *Cog. Sci.* 1981; 5:121-52.

[111] Bordage G, Connell KJ, Chang RW, Gecht MR, Sinacore JM. Assessing the semantic content of clinical case presentations: studies of reliability and concurrent validity. *Acad. Med.* 1997; 72(10 Suppl 1):S37-9.

[112] Bordage G. Elaborated knowledge: a key to successful diagnostic thinking. *Acad. Med.* 1994; 69(11):883-5.

[113] Eva K, Brooks L, Norman G. Does "Shortness of Breath" = "Dyspnea"?: The Biasing Effect of Feature Instantiation in Medical Diagnosis. *Academic Medicine.* 2001; 76(10):S11-3.

[114] Bordage G, Lemieux M. Semantic structures and diagnostic thinking of experts and novices. *Acad Med.* 1991; 66(9 Suppl):S70-2.

[115] Joseph GM, Patel VL. Domain knowledge and hypothesis generation in diagnostic reasoning. *Med. Decis Making.* 1990; 10(1):31-46.

[116] Rikers RM, Loyens SM, Schmidt HG. The role of encapsulated knowledge in clinical case representations of medical students and family doctors. *Med. Educ.* 2004 Oct; 38(10):1035-43.

[117] Harasym P, Papa F, Schumaker R. The structure of medical knowledge reflected in clinicians' disease estimates of the probabilities of signs/symptoms within diseases. In: Scherpbier A, van der Vleuten, CPM., Rethans, JJ and van der Steeg, AFW, ed. *Advances in Medical Education.* Dordrecht: Kluwer Academic Publishers 1997:602-7.

[118] Elstein AS, Kleinmuntz B, Rabinowitz M, McAuley R, Murakami J, Heckerling PS, et al. Diagnostic reasoning of high- and low-domain-knowledge clinicians: a reanalysis. *Med. Decis Making.* 1993; 13(1):21-9.

[119] Gale J, Marsden P. *Medical Diagnosis: From Student to Clinician.* Oxford: Oxford University Press; 1983.

[120] Gagne R. *The Conditions of Learning.* 2nd ed. London: Holt, Rinehart and Winston; 1973.

[121] Graesser A, Clark L. *Structures and Procedures of Implicit Knowledge.* Norwood, NJ: Ablex; 1985.

[122] Voss J, Bisanz G. Knowledge and the processing of narrative and expository texts. In: Britton B, Black J, eds. *Understanding Expository Text.* Hillsdale, NJ: Erlbaum; 1985:173-98.

[123] Muzzin L, Norman G, Feightner J, Tugwell P. Expertise in recall of clinical protocols in two specialty areas. *Proceedings of the 22nd Conference on Research in Medical Education*; 1983; Washington, DC; 1983.

[124] Patel V, Groen G. Non-monotonicity in novice-intermediate-expert comparisons. *Proceedings of the 27th Annual Conference of Research in Medical Education;* 1986; New Orleans, LA; 1986.

[125] Claessen HF, Boshuizen HP. Recall of medical information by students and doctors. *Med. Educ.* 1985; 19(1):61-7.

[126] Boshuizen H. The development of medical expertise: a cognitive-psychological approach [PhD]. Maastricht: University of Limburg; 1989.

[127] Patel VL, Groen GJ, Scott HM. Biomedical knowledge in explanations of clinical problems by medical students. *Med. Educ.* 1988; 22(5):398-406.

[128] Arocha J, Patel V. Use of Surface and Structural Relations in Diagnostic Problem Solving by Medical Trainees. Montreal, Canada: Centre for Medical Education, McGill University; 1991. Report No.: CME91-CS1.

[129] Trottier M, Patel V. Medical expertise and reasoning about laboratory tests. *Professions Education Researchers Notes.* 1986; 8:10-3.

[130] Dauphinee WD, Patel VL. Early career choice: an unsuccessful program. *J. Med. Educ.* 1983; 58(9):695-702.

[131] Patel V, Glaser R, Arocha J. Cognition and expertise: acquisition of medical competence. *Clin. Invest Med.* 2000; 23(4):256-60.

[132] Gentner D. Structure mapping: A theoretical framework for analogy. *Cognitive Science.* 1983; 7:155-70.

[133] Balla JI, Biggs JB, Gibson M, Chang AM. The application of basic science concepts to clinical problem-solving. *Med. Educ.* 1990; 24(2):137-47.

[134] Patel V, Evans D, Chawla A. Predictive versus diagnostic reasoning in the application of biomedical knowledge. 9th *Cognitive Science Society Annual Conference;* 1987; 1987.

[135] Kaufman D, Patel V. Interactive medical problem solving in the context of a clinical interview: the nature of expertise. *10th Annual Meeting of the Cognitive Science Society;* 1988; Hillsdale, NJ: Erlbaum; 1988.

[136] Patel VL, Evans DA, Groen GJ. Reconciling basic science and clinical reasoning. *Teaching and Learning in Medicine.* 1989:116-21.

[137] Lesgold A, Rubinson H, Feltovich P, Glaser R, Klopfer D. Expertise in a complex skill: diagnosing X-ray pictures. In: Chi M, Glaser, R and Farr, M, ed. *The Nature of Expertise.* Hillsdale, New Jersey: Lawrence Erlbaum Associates; 1988.

[138] Lesgold A. Acquiring expertise. In: Anderson J, Kosslyn S, eds. *Tutorials in Learning and Memory: Essays in Honour of Gordon Bower.* San Francisco: Freeman and Co; 1984.

[139] Kuipers B, Kassirer J. Causal reasoning in medicine: Analysis of a protocol. *Cog. Sci.* 1984; 8:363-85.

[140] Van der Wiel M, Boshuizen H, Schmidt H. Knowledge restructuring in expertise development: Evidence from pathophysiological representations of clinical cases by students and physicians. *European Journal of Cognitive Psychology.* 2000; 12(3):323-55.

[141] Lemieux M, Bordage G. Structuralisme et pedagogie medicale: etude comparative des strategies cognitives d'apprentis-mediecins. [A comparative study of the cognitive strategies of novice physicians]. *Recherches Semiotiques.* 1986; 6:143-79.

[142] Van der Wiel M, Boshuizen H. The explanation of clinical concepts by expert physicians, clerks and advanced students. *Teach Learn Med.* 1999; 11(3):153-63.

[143] Patel VL, Evans DA, Kaufman DR. Reasoning strategies and the use of biomedical knowledge by medical students. *Med. Educ.* 1990; 24(2):129-36.

[144] Boshuizen H, Schmidt H, Coughlin L. On the application of medical basic science knowledge in clinical reasoning: Implications for structural knowledge differences between experts and novices. *The Tenth Annual Conference of the Cognitive Science Society;* 1988; Montreal, Quebec, Canada; 1988. p. 517-23.

[145] Collins A. Generalising from situated knowledge in robust understanding. *Annual Conference of the American Educational Research Association;* 1990; Boston, MA; 1990.

[146] Patel V, Evans D, Groen G. Biomedical knowledge and clinical reasoning. In: Evans D, Patel V, eds. *Cognitive Science in Medicine.* Cambridge, MA: MIT Press; 1988.

[147] Hobus P, Boshuizen H, Schmidt H. Expert-novice differences in the role of contextual factors in early medical diagnosis. *Annual Meeting of the American Educational Research Association;* 1990; Boston; 1990.

[148] Hobus PP, Schmidt HG, Boshuizen HP, Patel VL. Contextual factors in the activation of first diagnostic hypotheses: expert-novice differences. *Med. Educ.* 1987; 21(6):471-6.

[149] Schmidt H, Boshuizen H, Norman G. Reflections on the nature of expertise in medicine. In: Keravnou E, ed. *Deep Models for Medical Knowledge Engineering.* Amsterdam: Elsevier, North-Holland; 1992:231-48.

[150] Norman G, Muzzin L, Rosenthal D. Expert-novice differences in perception and categorisation in dermatology. *Annual Meeting of the American Educational Research Association;* 1985; Chicago, Illinois; 1985.

[151] Norman GR, Brooks LR, Cunnington JP, Shali V, Marriott M, Regehr G. Expert-novice differences in the use of history and visual information from patients. *Acad. Med.* 1996; 71(10 Suppl):S62-4.

[152] Norman GR, Brooks LR, Regehr G, Marriott M, Shali V. Impact of feature interpretation on medical student diagnostic performance. *Acad. Med.* 1996; 71(1 Suppl):S108-9.

[153] Custers EJ, Boshuizen HP, Schmidt HG. The influence of medical expertise, case typicality, and illness script component on case processing and disease probability estimates. *Mem. Cognit.* 1996; 24(3):384-99.

[154] Custers P, Boshuizen H, Schmidt H. The relationship between medical expertise and the development of illness scripts. *Annual Meeting of the American Educational Research Association;* 1992; San Francisco, CA; 1992.

[155] Flavell J. Metacognition and cognitive monitoring: A new area of cognitive-developmental inquiry. *American Psychologist.* 1979; 34:906-11.

[156] Swanson H. Influence of metacognitive knowledge and aptitude on problem solving. *J. Educ. Psychol.* 1990; 82:306-14.

[157] Norman GR, Rosenthal D, Brooks LR, Allen SW, Muzzin LJ. The development of expertise in dermatology. *Arch Dermatol.* 1989; 125(8): 1063-8.

[158] Allen S, Brooks L, Norman G. Effect of prior examples on rule-based diagnostic performance. *Research in Medical Education: Proceedings of the 25th Annual Conference;* 1988; Washington, DC: Association of American Medical Colleges; 1988.

[159] Boshuizen H, Schmidt H, Custers E, van der Wiel M. Knowledge development and restructuring in the domain of medicine: the role of theory and practice. *Learning and Instruction.* 1995; 5:269-89.

[160] Boshuizen H, Schmidt H. The development of clinical reasoning expertise. In: Higgs J, Jones M, eds. *Clinical Reasoning in the Health Professions.* Oxford; Boston: Butterworth-Heinermann; 1995:24-32.

[161] Hassebrock F, Prietula M. A protocol-based coding scheme for the analysis of medical reasoning. *J. Man-machine Studies.* 1992; 37:613-52.

[162] Belleza F, Bower G. The representational and processing characteristics of scripts. *Bulletin of the Psychonomic Society.* 1981; 18:1-4.

[163] Patel V, Kaufman D. Clinical reasoning and biomedical knowledge: Implications for teaching. In: Higgs JJ, M, ed. *Clinical Reasoning in the Health Professions.* Oxford: Butterworth-Heinemann; 2000:33-44.

[164] Patel V, Groen G, Norman G. Reasoning and instruction in medical curricula. *Cogn. Instruct.* 1993; 10:133-39.

[165] Kintsch W. The role of knowledge in discourse comprehension: a construction-integration model. *Psychological Review.* 1988; 95:163-82.

[166] Anderson J. *The Architecture of Cognition*. Cambridge, MA: Harvard University Press; 1983.

[167] Norman G. The essential role of basic science in medical education: the perspective from psychology. *Clinical and Investigative Medicine*. 2000; 23(1):47-51.

[168] Coughlin L, Patel V. Text comprehension and expertise in the domain of medicine. *Annual Meeting of the American Educational Research Association;* 1986; San Francisco, CA; 1986.

[169] Boshuizen H, Schmidt H, Coughlin L. On-line representation of a clinical case and the development of expertise. *Annual meeting of the American Educational Research Association;* 1987; Washington, DC; 1987.

[170] Hopkins K, Stanley J, Hopkins B. *Educational and Psychological Measurement and Evaluation*. 7th edition ed. Needham heights, Massachusetts: Simon and Schuster, Inc; 1990.

[171] Newble D, Cannon R. Assessing the Students. *A Handbook for Medical Teachers*. 2nd edition ed. Norwell, Massachusetts: Kluwer Academic Publishers; 1987:85-115.

[172] Rimoldi H. The test of diagnostic skills. *Journal of Medical Education*. 1961; 36:73-9.

[173] Wass V, Van der Vleuten C, Shatzer J, Jones R. Assessment of clinical competence. *Lancet* 2001; 357(9260):945-9.

[174] Norcini JJ, Diserens D, Day SC, Cebul RD, Schwartz JS, Beck LH, et al. The scoring and reproducibility of an essay test of clinical judgment. *Acad. Med.* 1990; 65(9 Suppl):S41-2.

[175] Frijns P, van der Vleuten C, Verwijnen G, vam Leeuwen Y. The effect of structure in scoring methods of the reproducibility of tests using open-ended questions. In: Bender W, Hiemstra, RJ., Scherbier, AJJA., Zwierstra, RP, ed. *Teaching and Assessing Clinical Competence*. Gromingen: Boekwerk 1990:466-71.

[176] Fowell S, Bligh J. Recent developments in assessing medical students. *Postgraduate Medicine Journal*. 1998; 74:18-24.

[177] Helfer R, Slater C. Measuring the process of solving clinical diagnostic problems. *British Journal of Medical Education*. 1971; 5:48-52.

[178] Norman G, Feightner J. A comparison of behaviour on simulated patients and patient management problems. *Journal of Medical Education*. 1981; 55:529-37.

[179] Newble DI, Hoare J, Baxter A. Patient management problems. Issues of validity. *Med. Educ.* 1982; 16(3):137-42.

[180] Norman G, Bordage G, Curry L, al e. A review of recent innovations in assessment. In: Wakeford R, ed. *Directions in Clinical Assessment: Report of the First Cambridge Conference on the Assessment of Clinical Competence*. Cambridge, UK: Office of the Regius Professor of Physic, Cambridge University School of Clinical Medicine, Addenbrooke's Hospital; 1985:8-27.

[181] Marshall J. Assessment of problem-solving ability. *Med. Educ.* 1977; 11(5):329-34.

[182] de Graaff E, Post GJ, Drop MJ. Validation of a new measure of clinical problem-solving. *Med. Educ.* 1987; 21(3):213-8.

[183] Van der Vleuten C, Swanson D. Assessment of clinical skills with standardised patients: the state of the art. *Teach Learn Med.* 1990; 2(2):58-76.

[184] Berner E, Hamilton L, Best W. A new approach ot evaluating problem solving in medical students. *Journal of Medical Education.* 1974; 49:666-72.

[185] Hodgkin K, Knox J. *Problem Centred Learning: The Modified Essay Question in Medical Education.* Edinburgh: Churchill Livingstone 1975.

[186] Feletti GI, Engel CE. The modified essay question for testing problem-solving skills. *Med. J. Aust.* 1980; 1(2):79-80.

[187] Neufeld V, Norman G. *Assessing Clinical Competence.* New York: Springer; 1985.

[188] de Graaff E. Simulation of Initial Medical Problem-solving: a test for the assessment of medical problem-solving. *Medical Teacher.* 1988; 10:49-55.

[189] Bransford J, Sherwood R, Vye N, Reiser J. Teaching thinking and problem solving. *American Psychologist.* 1986; 41:1078-89.

[190] Page G, Bordage G. The Medical Council of Canada's key features project: a more valid written examination of clinical decision-making skills. *Acad. Med.* 1995; 70(2):104-10.

[191] Page G, Bordage G, Allen T. Developing key-feature problems and examinations to assess clinical decision-making skills. *Acad. Med.* 1995; 70(3):194-201.

[192] Bordage G, Page G. An alternative approach to PMPs: the "key features" concept. In: Hart I, Harden R, eds. *Further Developments in Assessing Clinical Competence.* Montreal: Can-Heal Publications; 1987:57-75.

[193] Neville AJ, Cunnington J, Norman GR. Development of clinical reasoning exercises in a problem-based curriculum. *Acad. Med.* 1996; 71(1):S105-S7.

[194] Wood T, Cunnington J, Norman G. Assessing the measurement properties of a clinical reasoning exercise. *Teaching and Learning in Medicine.* 2000; 12(4):196-200.

[195] Charlin B, Roy L, Brailovsky C, Goulet F, van der Vleuten C. The Script Concordance test: a tool to assess the reflective clinician. *Teach Learn Med.* 2000 Fall; 12(4):189-95.

[196] Charlin B, Desaulniers M, Gagnon R, Blouin D, van der Vleuten C. Comparison of an aggregate scoring method with a consensus scoring method in a measure of clinical reasoning capacity. *Teach Learn Med.* 2002 Summer; 14(3):150-6.

[197] Bland AC, Kreiter CD, Gordon JA. The psychometric properties of five scoring methods applied to the script concordance test. *Acad. Med.* 2005 Apr; 80(4):395-9.

[198] Groves M, Scott I, Alexander H. Assessing clinical reasoning: a method to monitor its development in a PBL curriculum. *Med. Teach.* 2002 Sep; 24(5):507-15.

[199] Vu NV, Dawson-Saunders B, Barrows HS. Use of a medical reasoning aptitude test to help predict performance in medical school. *J. Med. Educ.* 1987; 62(4):325-35.

[200] Bordage G, Grant J, Marsden P. Quantitative assessment of diagnostic ability. *Med. Educ.* 1990; 24(5):413-25.

[201] Round AP. Teaching clinical reasoning - a preliminary controlled study. *Medical Education.* 1999; 33(7):480-3.

[202] Sobral DT. Diagnostic ability of medical students in relation to their learning characteristics and preclinical background. *Med. Educ.* 1995; 29 (4): 278-82.

[203] Jones UF. The reliability and validity of the Bordage, Grant and Marsden diagnostic thinking inventory for use with physiotherapists. *Medical Teacher.* 1997; 19(2):133-40.

[204] Beullens J, Struyf E, Van Damme B. Diagnostic ability in relation to clinical seminars and extended-matching questions examinations. *Med. Educ.* 2006 Dec; 40(12):1173-9.

[205] de Groot A. *Thought and Choice and Chess.* Den Haag: Mouton and Cie 1965.

[206] Patel V, Arocha J. Methods in the Study of Clinical Reasoning. In: Higgs J, Jones M, eds. *Clinical Reasoning in the Health Professions.* Oxford; Boston: Butterworth-Heinemann; 1995:35-48.

[207] Kassirer JP, Kuipers BJ, Gorry GA. Toward a theory of clinical expertise. *Am. J. Med.* 1982; 73(2):251-9.

[208] Coughlin LD, Patel VL. Processing of critical information by physicians and medical students. *J. Med. Educ.* 1987; 62(10):818-28.

[209] Chang RW, Bordage G, Connell KJ. The importance of early problem representation during case presentations. *Acad. Med.* 1998; 73(10 Suppl): S109-11.

[210] Newble D, Raymond G. Clinical memory as a potential measure of clinical problem solving ability. In: Harden R, Hart I, Mulholland H, eds. *Approaches to the Assessment of Clinical Competence, Part 1.* Dundee: Centre for Medical Education 1992:347-51.

[211] Elstein AS. Clinical problem solving and decision psychology: comment on "The epistemology of clinical reasoning" [In Process Citation]. *Acad. Med.* 2000; 75(10 Suppl):S134-6.

[212] Norman GR, Schmidt HG. Effectiveness of problem-based learning curricula: theory, practice and paper darts. *Med. Educ.* 2000; 34(9):721-8.

[213] Lyon HC, Jr., Healy JC, Bell JR, O'Donnell JF, Shultz EK, Moore-West M, et al. PlanAlyzer, an interactive computer-assisted program to teach clinical problem solving in diagnosing anemia and coronary artery disease. *Acad. Med.* 1992; 67(12):821-8.

[214] Myers J, Dorsey J. Using *Diagnostic Reasoning (DxR)* to teach and evaluate clinical reasoning skills. *Academic Medicine.* 1994; 69(5):428-9.

[215] Mackel JV, Farris H, Mittman BS, Wilkes M, Kanouse DE. A Windows-based tool for the study of clinical decision-making. *Medinfo.* 1995; 8 Pt 2:1687.

[216] Friedman CP, Elstein AS, Wolf FM, Murphy GC, Franz TM, Heckerling PS, et al. Enhancement of clinicians' diagnostic reasoning by computer-based consultation: a multisite study of 2 systems. *JAMA.* 1999; 282(19):1851-6.

[217] Schuwirth LWT, van der Vleuten CPM, de Kock CA, Peperkamp AGW, Donkers H. Computerized case-based testing: A modern method to assess clinical decision making. *Medical Teacher.* 1996; 18(4):294-9.

[218] Rendas A, Pinto PR, Gamboa T. A computer simulation designed for problem-based learning. *Med Educ.* 1999; 33(1):47-54.

[219] Friedman CP. Anatomy of the clinical simulation. *Acad. Med.* 1995; 70(3):205-9.

[220] Schuwirth L. Can clinical reasoning be taught or can it only be learned? *Med. Educ.* 2002 Aug; 36(8):695-6.

[221] Woods NN, Brooks LR, Norman GR. The value of basic science in clinical diagnosis: creating coherence among signs and symptoms. *Med. Educ.* 2005 Jan; 39(1):107-12.

[222] Ark TK, Brooks LR, Eva KW. Giving learners the best of both worlds: do clinical teachers need to guard against teaching pattern recognition to novices? *Acad Med.* 2006 Apr; 81(4):405-9.

[223] Bowen JL. Educational strategies to promote clinical diagnostic reasoning. *The New England journal of medicine.* 2006 Nov 23; 355(21):2217-25.

[224] Eva KW. What every teacher needs to know about clinical reasoning. *Med. Educ.* 2005 Jan; 39(1):98-106.

[225] Newble DI. Assessing clinical competence at the undergraduate level. *Med. Educ.* 1992; 26(6):504-11.

[226] Norman G. Building on experience--the development of clinical reasoning. *The New England journal of medicine.* 2006 Nov 23; 355(21):2251-2.

Index

C

Canada, 52, 69, 74, 75, 78
candidates, 62
capacity, 37, 49, 59, 79
cardiovascular system, 26
causal model, 7
causal reasoning, 4, 6, 40
causal relationship, 21
causality, 67
Chicago, 75
chunking, 20, 41
classes, 28
classical, 17
classification, 14, 70
classified, 13, 30, 46
clinical, vii, 1, 2, 3, 4, 5, 6, 7, 9, 10, 11, 12,
    13, 14, 15, 16, 17, 18, 19, 20, 21, 24, 25,
    26, 27, 28, 29, 30, 31, 32, 33, 34, 35, 36,
    37, 38, 39, 40, 41, 42, 43, 45, 46, 47, 48,
    49, 50, 51, 52, 53, 54, 55, 56, 57, 58, 59,
    61, 62, 66, 67, 68, 69, 70, 71, 72, 73, 74,
    75, 76, 77, 78, 79, 80, 81
clinical case representation, 73
clinical diagnosis, 70, 81
clinical examination, 62
clinical judgment, 77
clinical presentation, 11, 67
clinical years, 62
clinician(s), 4, 5, 9, 10, 11, 12, 13, 18, 17, 20,
    24, 25, 27, 30, 34, 35, 38, 39, 41, 42, 48,
    54, 56, 58
closure, 11
clustering, 37
clusters, 37, 41
coding, 76
cognition, 1, 3, 5, 24, 35, 51
cognitive, 1, 9, 12, 13, 21, 24, 25, 35, 48, 49,
    51, 54, 56, 58, 65, 68, 70, 71, 74, 75, 76
cognitive ability, 24, 25, 35
cognitive level, 49
cognitive perspective, 65
cognitive process, 12, 48, 49, 51, 54, 56, 58

cognitive psychology, 25, 56, 71
coherence, 6, 11, 33, 61, 81
communication, 35, 45, 47
community, 63
compassion, 35
competence, 23, 43, 45, 48, 50, 51, 52, 63, 69,
    72, 74, 77, 81
complementary, 6
complexity, 3, 6, 14, 17, 31, 54, 58
components, 24, 28, 30, 34, 38, 45, 51
composition, 38
comprehension, 57, 76, 77
computer, 15, 49, 59, 62, 69, 80
computer simulations, 15
concrete, 26, 32
Concurrent validity, 46
confidence, 58
confusion, 32
consciousness, 58
consensus, 53, 79
consolidation, 21
constraints, 32, 40
construct validity, 45, 46, 47, 51, 52, 53, 55,
    69
Construct validity, 46
construction, 31, 33, 38, 76
consultants, 29
Content validity, 46
context-dependent, 1, 6, 12, 16, 17, 26
continuing, 11
control, 35, 51
coordination, 66
coronary artery disease, 80
correlation, 13, 25, 47, 50, 52
cost-benefit analysis, 66
covering, 37
credibility, 6
Criterion-related validity, 46
critical thinking, 46
cross-sectional, 69
cues, 10, 11, 20, 34, 51, 55, 59
cultural, 13
curriculum, vii, 2, 67, 78, 79

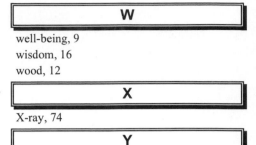